The $ales Slump Doctor Is In!

The First-Ever Scientifically Tested Method For Ending The Sales Slump.

Mickey M. Greenfield, J.D., Ph.D.
THE SALES SLUMP DOCTOR

Lexington House

Publishers of Leading American Books and References Since 1965

The Sales Slump Doctor Is In!
This publication is designed to provide accurate and authoritative information in regard to the subject matter covered. It is published with the understanding that the publisher and author are not engaged in rendering legal, accounting, or other professional service. If legal advice or other professional advice, including financial, is required, the services of a competent professional person should be sought.
—**From a declaration of Principles, jointly adopted by a Committee of the American Bar Association and a Committee of Publishers.**

Copyright © 2001 By Mickey M. Greenfield, J.D., Ph.D.
First Edition.
Lexington House ® books are available through most USA bookstores. They can also be ordered from the publisher at the below address.

All rights reserved under International and Pan-American Copyright Conventions. No part of this book may be reproduced or transmitted in any form or by any means electronic, or mechanical, including photocopying, recording, or by any information storage and retrieval system, without expressed permission in writing from the publisher.

Published by *Lexington House* ®, 98 Dennis Drive, Lexington, KY 40503 USA.
Publisher of Leading American Books and References Since 1965.
Visit our helpful web site at www.kisslingorganization.com.

Printed in the United States of America on acid-free paper.
Editorial Direction, Copy Editing and Design by Heather Wade, assisted by Karin Stritzke and Emily K. Hendren.
Distributed to the trade by the Alliance Book Company.

The stylized nomenclature reading *Lexington House* ® is composed of a modified version of SheerGrace typeface and is depicted with a classic building structure enclosed in a semi-circle extending from the first letter of the first word. This is a registered trademark of *Lexington House* ®.

Publishers of the following three best-selling series:
Profiling America's Three Greatest® - ***Quick Guide***® - **100 Secrets**®

Library of Congress Cataloging-in-Publication Data
Greenfield, Mickey M.
  The Sales Slump Doctor Is In! 1st Ed.
      p.   cm.
ISBN 0-910882-03-7
  1. Sales
  2. Psychology
  3. Training
  4. Self-Help
  5. Mickey M. Greenfield, J.D., Ph.D.

Quantity Discounts Available
Lexington House titles are available at special quantity discounts for bulk purchases by governments, businesses, associations, schools, corporations, religious organizations and for other groups. For **FREE** detailed information please write to:
Special Volume Discount Sales Department

Lexington House ®
98 Dennis Drive
Lexington, Kentucky 40503 USA

DEDICATION

This book is dedicated to my beautiful wife, Sonia, my gorgeous daughters, Sharon, Lori, and Tina, and my wonderful grandchildren, Tova, Kuyanna, Devin, Jacob, and Matthew. It would not have been possible without their love, support, and understanding.

A special thanks goes to my brother, Stanley, who gave me the courage to proceed with this project.

And then there is Jacque O'Malley O'Neal who, when she was with Maccabees Mutual, published me for the very first time, and when she was with CNA, gave me my very first paid speaking engagement. Without her early support and encouragement none of this would have gotten off the ground. I have lost touch with her, but would appreciate word from any of you if you know how I can locate her.

I would also like to thank the many people who helped gather information, do research, and who gave their support. But most of all, I want to thank the many salespeople who let me learn from their misfortunes by letting me treat them. Thanks.

TABLE OF CONTENTS

Introduction	Rev. Dr. John Clements	
Foreword	David K. "Straight Shooter" Straight	
Chapter 1 –	Another Week Without a Sale: *How I Discovered the Secret for Ending the Sales Slump.*	1
Chapter 2 –	How the Mystery of Using Balancing Factors Got Me Out of My Slump.	10
Chapter 3 –	How You, Too, Can End Your Sales Slumps.	18
Chapter 4 –	How Do You Get People in Sales Slumps To Talk? You Listen, Listen, Listen. *This Also Works Like Magic In Sales Interviews.*	28
Chapter 5 –	How Forming Your Own Board of Directors Will Solve Your Prospecting Woes. *(Or, The Lord Helps Those Who Help Themselves.)*	35
Chapter 6 –	Pain! The Greatest Gift God Gave To Sales Managers.	40
Chapter 7 –	Motivation – A Short-Term Fix For A Long-Term Problem.	48
Chapter 8 –	You Can Live Through a Hostile Takeover and Merger and Come Out Whole.	53
Chapter 9 –	The Rippling Effect That Sales Slumps Have On Our Economy.	63
Chapter 10 –	Stages of Slump Intervention, and What They Mean to the Sales Manager.	66
Chapter 11 –	Forrest Wallace Cato Interviews The Sales Slump Doctor.	71
Appendix A		79
Appendix B		84
Bonus Workbook	If You Can't Say It, You Can't Sell It!	
Workbook Appendix		24
About the Author		33

INTRODUCTION

THE SALES SLUMP DOCTOR IS IN! The first-ever scientifically tested method for ending the sales slump. Isn't that powerful? Imagine, a scientifically tested method to help you get out of your sales slump, and it has nothing to do with motivation. He talks about pain being one of the most paradoxical things God placed on this earth. He explains that in his slump intervention techniques you either use the pain or it will use you. I didn't believe that any of this could be possible until I read this book. And it's so e-a-s-y to learn to use. This book will change your life!

Dr. Mickey Greenfield, affectionately called THE SALES SLUMP DOCTOR by the many salespeople he has helped, began his career selling sparklers from a cardboard box that he made into a stand where he could display his wares. He was five years old. Then, he didn't know the word slump – He had cute golden ringlets, and he sold out of sparklers everyday. What could be better? It wasn't until he was selling life insurance that he experienced sales slumps. Oh, he was considered by all to be successful. After all, he was a Life and Qualifying Member of the Million Dollar Round Table, but few knew his frustration. As he described it to me, he was either on top of the world or in the depths of Hades. There was very little middle ground. He was collecting a five-figure commission for the month or nothing.

He went back to school to study psychology while maintaining a full time job selling life insurance. He had to have income. His three daughters were in private schools, and his wife was attending graduate studies with him.

While Greenfield was studying abnormal psychology, his professor was describing the effects of a crisis on a person's life, and Dr. Greenfield immediately saw this as a sales slump. After some discussion with the professor, they both concluded that a crisis and a sales slump were the same.

Meanwhile, Dr. Greenfield began helping salespeople who were experiencing sales slumps with a tried-and-true procedure know as crisis intervention. It worked, but there was no way of knowing whether it was the crisis intervention technique or some charisma possessed by Dr. Greenfield. When he was studying for his Ph.D. in psychology and had to write his dissertation, he decided to test his theory that crisis intervention techniques are effective in ending a sales slump. It was successful and, thus far, has been the only scientifically tested research on the sales slump.

In *The Sales Slump Doctor Is In,* Dr. Greenfield begins with a chapter describing his discovery and the research to support his discovery. That's followed by two chapters giving detailed examples of what the slump intervention techniques are and how to use them. Then he gets into the role communication plays in helping someone in a sales slump grow beyond the problems continuing the sales slump. Self-help methods are discussed in the next chapter. This is where he describes one of the most unique Board of Directors that I have ever read about. He then shows how the pain caused by the sales slump can become your ally if you know how to use it. A short chapter follows on why motivation historically has failed to keep good salespeople out of sales slumps. Then he takes a look at how slump intervention plays a role in helping with hostile takeovers. Naturally, he discusses how a lost dollar due to sales slumps affects the economy, and finally, he re-examines and defines the stages of slump intervention.

The Bonus Workbook is devoted entirely to communication skills: how they are used to alleviate the sales slump and to train trainers to teach slump intervention techniques to salespeople and salesmanagers around the world.

Finally, it should be pointed out that Dr. Greenfield's book, while directed at sales, is applicable to solving many other life problems, such as coping with the different stages of life and dealing with psychological trauma, interpersonal problems, and all forms of crises.

John Clements

Rev. Dr. John Clements is well-known, being England's best-selling inspirational writer and a traveler who speaks in many countries across the world. A resident of Norwich, England, Clements wrote the international best-selling books **Make Your Walls Tumble, Stained Glass Wisdom,** and other critically acclaimed works. He authored the course **Sales Training For the Non-Sales Professional.**

FOREWORD

By David K. "Straight Shooter" Straight

Up front, even before you ask, I will immediately answer your question about Dr. Mickey M. Greenfield! Before you finish reading this valuable book, you will most likely want to know the answer. So here is your answer in advance.

Yes! You can contact Dr. Mickey M. Greenfield and talk about your sales situation or obtain details about arranging for him to speak to your group. Dr. Greenfield routinely performs professional consultations and makes platform presentations for people or groups concerned with improving sales.

Here are the contact details you may need:

> Mickey M. Greenfield, JD, Ph.D.
> The Greenfield Center
> 1820 Barrs Street
> Suite 640
> Jacksonville, Florida 32204
> phone: 904-389-3784; fax: 904-389-4618
> e-mail: mgreen1932@aol.com

Don't hesitate to contact Dr. Greenfield. There is no obligation to you. It is very possible that your sales slump can also be cured. One of Dr. Greenfield's great joys in life is when sales professionals, sales trainers, and others come backstage or write and phone to inform him of how his breakthrough work has enabled them to overcome their sales slumps and reach record sales achievements.

This book can help you make similar advancements. Among the immortal names in the sales profession is the author of this book. Dr. Mickey M. Greenfield, in writing *The Sales Slump Doctor Is In!*, proves within these pages something his clients well know. And his clients are global and range from **Fortune 500** corporations to small independent five-person operations. Here Dr. Greenfield proves that in most cases the sales slump can be totally cured. As you read, please make notes on these pages since this information is more valuable than money itself.

David K. Straight
Author, *Straight Shooter Selling* and
Dream Homes and Your Financial Victory

BOOK I

YOUR SALES SLUMP

CHAPTER 1

Another Week Without a Sale.
How I Discovered the Secret for Ending the Sales Slump

Another week without a sale – I can't even get an appointment. What's going to happen next week? The car payment is due. The mortgage payment is due. My whole world is crashing!

The home office calls wanting to know whether I'm still working. Their point is simple – produce or we'll get someone who will!

My faithful Girl Friday rushes in to tell me another appointment has been canceled – something about his banker said he didn't need it. Am I paranoid? Maybe they really are out to get me. My confidence shot, I leave the office for "a short one" with the boys, and to avoid another call from my banker. One leads to another, but even four Silver Bullets haven't dulled the fear. The alcohol is even more depressing.

When I hit the door of the house, Sonia and the three babies are ready to charge me and begin the usual contest to see who can make me yell "shut up" first. Sonia is demanding my support as well as an attentive ear, and all the while, Sharon, Lori and Tina are vying for the attention of Daddy, the only male in the house. I want to turn around, go back to the club and have four more – only this time doubles!

I can't tell Sonia my problems – she has her own. I really need to help her, but how can I help another when I can't even help myself! So, instead of talking to her I become even more withdrawn, and a big case of guilt begins to grow. I feel guilty because I can't give my family what I think they want; I feel guilty because I can't give Sonia the kind of moral support she deserves; I feel guilty because I let everyone down. I wish I could die! Failing this, too, I drink myself into oblivion.

It's morning again. I stop by the coffee shop, being careful not to get there when my banker is having his usual morning cup. When you have to start the day like this, it's usually down hill from there on.

In the office I try to use the phone to set up appointments, but I am afraid to call the prospects. If they say no, where can I turn? Meanwhile, the secretary is holding my calls so I can devote all my attention to contacting prospects. I am not calling prospects, and if by chance a prospect tries to contact me, he is told I am out. What a self-defeating situation!

The more I sit in my office with the world shut out, the more I become afraid of what that world is going to do to me. The longer I put off calling prospects, the more frightened I am of them.

Fortunately, time passes, and once again I go to the club for a "shooter" with the boys. One becomes four or five, and it's time again to face Sonia and the girls – to face them, not as a winner, but as the loser I am becoming. What can I do? Can someone help? Will anyone help?

Fifteen years and at least fifty slumps later, I decided to enter graduate studies in psychology. In an introductory course, Dr. Bach said "When a person faces a problem he cannot solve, he has a rise in inner tension with signs of anxiety and an inability to function in extended periods of emotional upset." He called this condition a crisis, but I immediately saw it as a slump. Needless to say, my ears perked up and the good doctor had my complete and undivided attention. Did psychologists know something about the slump – the condition that has plagued salespeople since before Moses tried to sell the children of Israel the Ten Commandments?

After class I cornered Dr. Bach to get more information. I ended up with him across the table at dinner, which extended into the wee hours of the morning. When we parted, we were both convinced that the term *slump* and the term *crisis* were synonymous. This sent me on a search of the literature, which, in addition to confirming my feelings that these conditions were the same, taught me how to treat the slump just as you can treat other psychological conditions. Eureka! I had discovered the wheel!

I wanted to subject my theory, that crisis intervention techniques would be effective in reversing the negative effects salespeople experience during the sales slump, to scientific research. So, when I entered my doctoral studies, I decided to write my dissertation on that very subject. Before I could begin the research, I needed to gain access to salespeople who were suffering sales slumps. To accomplish this, I contacted the program chairman for the local General Agents and Managers Association (GAMA) in Savannah, Georgia, and requested an opportunity to speak at their next meeting. He was most gracious and made it possible for me to do just that.

I then explained to this group that I needed enough salespeople suffering from sales slumps to comprise three groups: **Control Group 1,** made up of agents who would not know they are being observed and would remain anonymous to me; **Control Group 2,** made up of agents who would be seen by me; and the **Experimental Group,** made up of agents in sales slumps who would be seen by me and treated with crisis intervention techniques. They all had to be full-time agents with at least three years of experience selling insurance. If they did not weed themselves out of the business within three years, I knew they were dedicated and knew how to sell. The general agents and managers gave me their support, and agents experiencing sales slumps were forthcoming.

All of the salespeople in Control Group 2 and the Experimental Group were self-selected; that is, each salesperson chose to become part of the research, and all were seen during the initial active phase of their sales slump except for two salespeople in Control Group 2, who began their sales slump the prior month. The recovery month calculations represent the month immediately following participation in the experiment. The salespeople's general agents or managers furnished all calculations.

The salespeople were given a random number according to their order of arrival at my office. Odd-numbered salespeople were assigned to the Experimental Group, and even-numbered salespeople were assigned to Control Group 2. None of these salespeople were known to me prior to this research.

Members of Control Group 2 scheduled their own appointments and were seen individually for five sessions, each session lasting at least 30 minutes. All were seen daily except one salesperson who had a one-day break between one of his sessions. At the initial session, all were asked to complete a questionnaire, received instructions as to the four psychological tests they would be taking, and then completed the first test. At subsequent sessions, each person completed another psychological test, and the results of the previous test were discussed. At the final session, the results from the last psychological test were discussed, and all their previous tests were summarized. Each person was individually thanked and asked to return in one month's time with their sales results. All returned in the one month allocated time frame with their sales figures. The participants were given a complete explanation of the significance of their participation in the experiment, and were offered crisis intervention techniques if they were still experiencing a sales slump. No subjects took advantage of this offer, nor did any indicate that they were still experiencing a sales slump.

The Experimental Group's salespeople also scheduled their own appointments, and were seen individually for five sessions, each session lasting at least 30 minutes. All subjects were seen daily except one who had a two-day break between one of her sessions. At the initial session, all salespeople were asked to complete the same questionnaire that Control Group 2 completed, and received instructions regarding the four psychological tests they would be taking. (Identical tests that were given to Control Group 2.) They completed the first test, and then were interviewed using crisis intervention techniques. These techniques were:

> **1.** Discover whether the salesperson had a realistic perception of the events relating to the sales slump occurring at the present time;

2. Discover whether the salesperson had adequate situational support;
3. Discover whether the salesperson had adequate coping skills to overcome the present problem.

When the interview revealed a problem in one of these areas, and all the interviews did, I would help the salesperson work through the problem. Examples of this are discussed later in this chapter. The testing procedure was identical to the procedure utilized with Control Group 2. At the end of the fifth session, subjects were individually thanked and asked to return in one month with their sales results.

Control Group 1 salespeople were not seen, nor were they aware they were involved in the study. Their respective general agents and managers supplied the raw sales data. The subjects remained anonymous except for their sales figures. The general agents and managers, after explaining the purpose of the research, obtained the consent of each person prior to releasing the data to me. The instruments used for the psychological testing held no significant importance other than their value as a placebo for Control Group 2. This group of tests was selected based on the following criteria:

1. The tests had to be cost-effective.
2. The tests had to be self-administered.
3. The tests had to have a reading level of no greater than the seventh grade.
4. The tests required no longer than 10 to 15 minutes to complete.

DATA DISCUSSION

The statistical testing[2] supported the following conclusions:

1. That crisis intervention techniques significantly affected the overall recovery from the sales slump.
2. That salespeople recovered as a function of the treatment.
3. That salespeople recovered at different rates.

Therefore, the data supports the conclusion that crisis intervention techniques restore salespeople to their previous level of effectiveness prior to their sales slumps. It was more effective than the methods used in the two Control Groups.

Two alternative methods of examining the data conclusions are the mean percentage change from the base month through the slump and into the recovery, and the premium dollars generated during this same period. Figure 1.1 graphically exhibits the mean changes within each group in percentages from the base month. Control Group 1 began at 100% (the base month), dropped to 20% of the base month during the slump month, and only recovered to 88% of the base month. Control Group 2 began at 100%, dropped only to 64%, and recovered at 117% of the base month. The Experimental Group likewise began at 100%, dropped to 51% during the slump, and recovered at 154% of the base month.

Control Group 2's 17% recovery over base can be attributed to the Hawthorne effect. This is a phenomenon where the participants in an experiment improve simply because they are being observed.

The 54% increase over the base month demonstrated in the Experimental Group is significant statistically at the <.001 level. (See Figure 1.1)

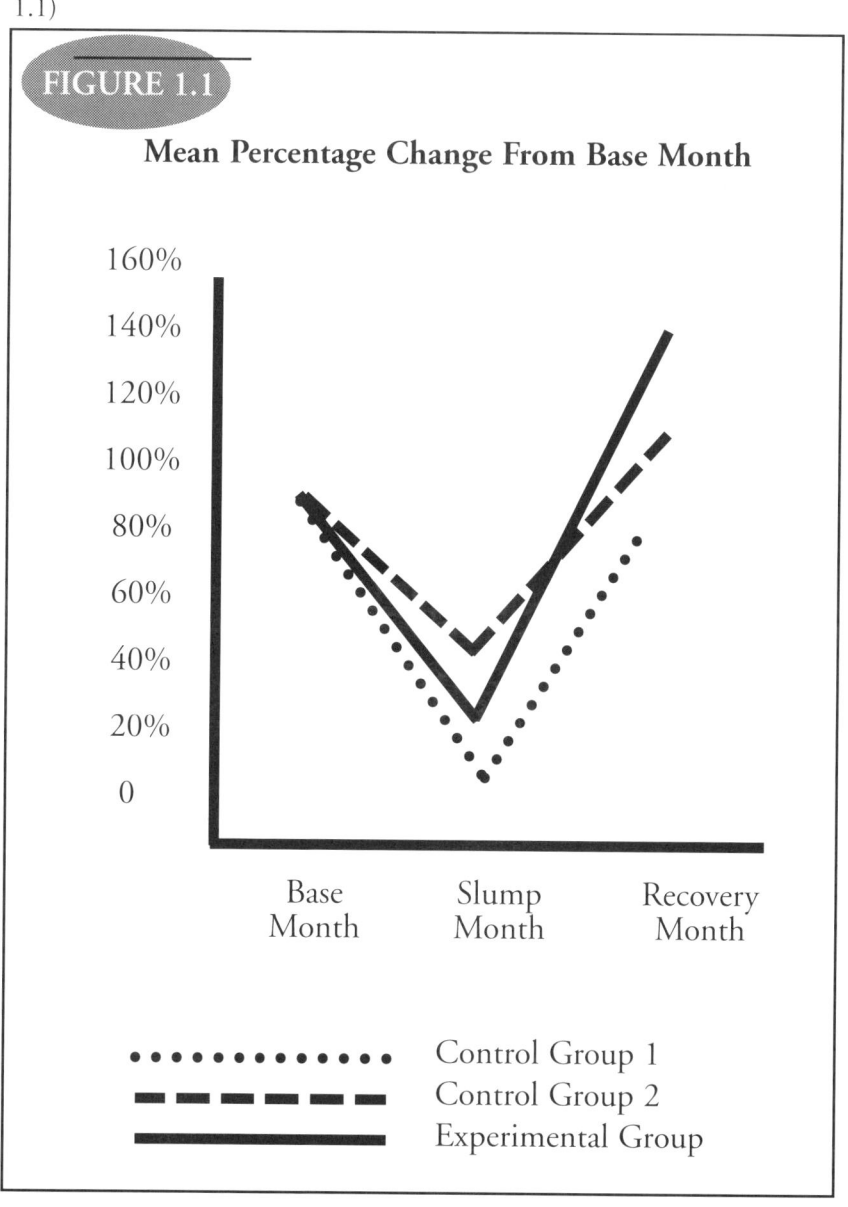

FIGURE 1.1

Mean Percentage Change From Base Month

•••••••••••••• Control Group 1
━ ━ ━ ━ ━ ━ Control Group 2
━━━━━━━━━━ Experimental Group

Figure 1.2 dramatically demonstrates the effect of this experiment in mean premium dollars produced during the base month, the slump month, and the recovery month for each group.

Control Group 1's mean base month was $1,754.67, the mean slump month was $354.83 (a typical, but drastic drop in production), and the mean recovery month came up to $1,543.83 ($210.84 below the mean base month). This is typical of the history of the salespeople I have seen in my private practice, who describe their prior sales slumps where no intervention was used.

Control Group 2's mean base month was $1,450.11, the mean slump month was $931.93 (a drop far less than Control Group 1 experienced), and the mean recovery month came up to $1,705.69 ($255.58 above the mean base month). This increase above the base month is attributed to the Hawthorne effect explained earlier.

The Experimental Group's mean base month was $3,793.64, the mean slump month was $1,935.41, and the mean recovery month came up to $5,824.43; a $2,030.79 recovery above the base month. (See Figure 1.2).

The raw data reflects a much higher Base Month for the Experimental Group than those of the Control Groups. However, change was measured in percentage increase from the Base Month to the Recovery Month, and, dollar values notwithstanding, the Experimental Group increased by 54%, while Control Group 1 reflected a minus 12% change from the Base Month and Control Group 2 reflected a 17% increase from the Base Month.

The data supports the hypothesis that crisis intervention techniques are effective in returning salespeople to their former level of effectiveness in selling. However, I would like to see a study replicating this present study where funds could be made available to allow a researcher the time and resources necessary to study a larger sample. Then, perhaps subjects could be stratified according to age, educational level, years of selling experience, etc.

Another need made apparent by this study is the need for a concise definition of the term *sales slump*. The lack of an exact definition compounds the problem of doing research on the sales slump, because one does not know exactly what other researchers are discussing when they use the term. Literature on sales is as bountiful as grains of sand on a beach – literature with concise and consistent definitions of sales slumps is as rare as diamonds.

When most writers discuss the sales slump, they assume the definition to be known *a priori*, and they universally discuss motivation as a means of overcoming the sales slump. Kilpatrick, et al[3], state that "Current literature on motivation reveals disagreement about its nature." When you take an undefined subject, the sales slump, and treat it with a disputed solution, motivation, you compound the unknown.

FIGURE 1.2

Mean Dollar Change From Base Month, Slump Month & Recovery Month

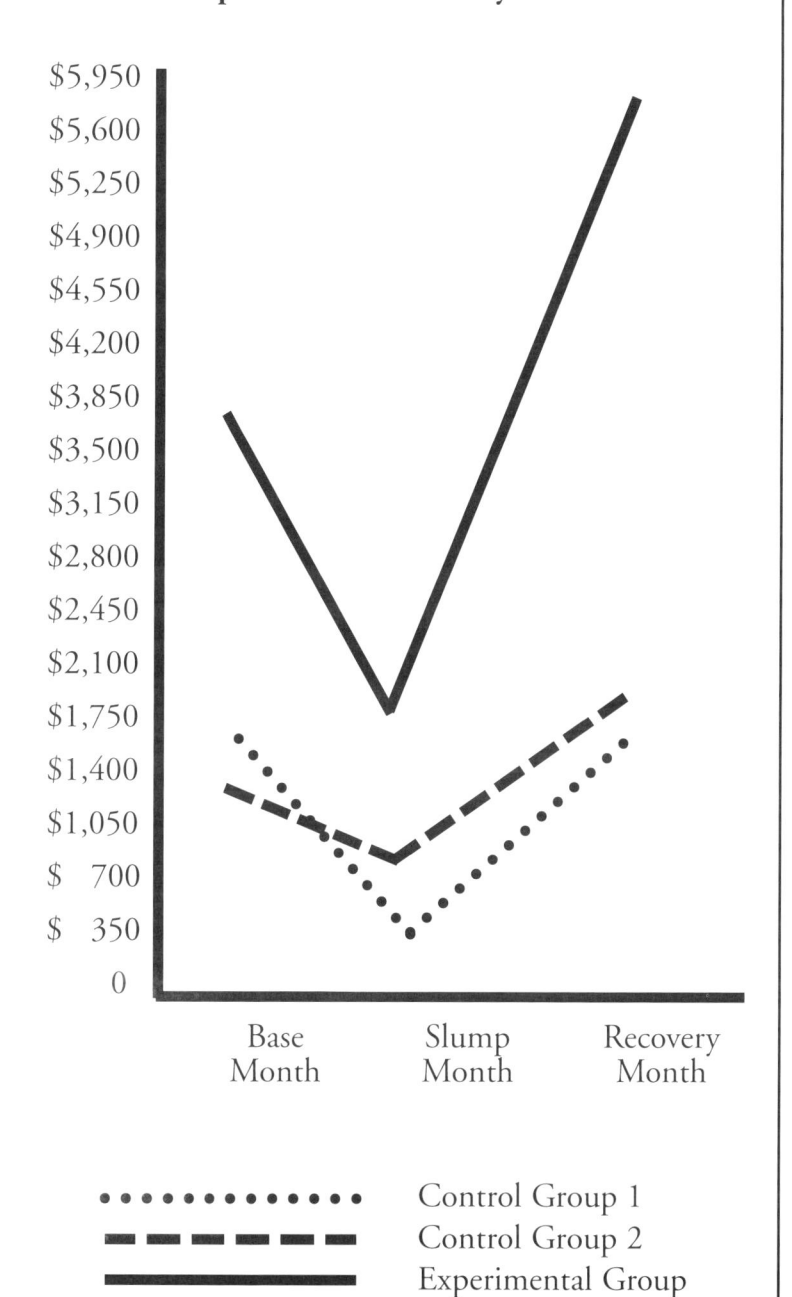

- • • • • • • • • • • • • • Control Group 1
- ― ― ― ― ― Control Group 2
- ───────── Experimental Group

When I first published articles on the subject of the sales slump[4] I was faced with the task of defining the term. As an operational definition, I said:

A sales slump occurs when a salesperson functions in a capacity below his normal level of effectiveness relative to selling. There is a rise in inner tension; anxiety levels rise; and he cannot function over an extended period of time.

This definition grew out of my fifteen years of experiencing sales slumps, my Acre of Diamonds.

Other than my own articles published earlier, there is no literature suggesting the utilization of crisis intervention for salespeople in sales slumps.

The literature on crisis intervention techniques is rather specific, and one should have no difficulty following its development from Freud through the current models. The model used in this study is Caplan's model[5] of crisis intervention, which utilizes the three balancing factors: 1) a realistic perception of the stressful event in our current situation; 2) adequate situational support (support from our environment, i.e., friends, family, work, etc.); and 3) adequate coping mechanisms. With the presence of these three balancing factors, equilibrium is maintained, and the crisis/slump is averted.

When one distorts their perception of reality they are looking without actually seeing that which is. When I was selling life insurance sometimes I perceived my inability to obtain appointments as a personal rejection, and would cease trying to get appointments. In the business this is termed "callitis." Usually, this failure to obtain appointments was merely poor prospecting. The perception that the prospects rejected me was a distortion, and caused me to focus on a non-existing problem instead of my poor prospecting – the real problem.

One of the salespeople in the Experimental Group stated that he could not sell during July and August because it was too hot. The subject was a combination agent who had to go out into the field each day to collect premiums. I agreed with him that July and August are too hot, and pointed out that he had to be out in the weather anyway, and, because of the extreme heat, he deserved more money. I further pointed out that commission salespeople give themselves raises, and didn't he think, because of the extreme heat that he had to experience, that he deserved more rather than less money for his efforts? This reframing changed his distorted view of his reality, and allowed him to recover from his slump with an approximate $3,000 increase over his base month. This salesperson was really convinced that he could not sell in July and August, and behaved accordingly. The results obviously proved this to be a distortion of reality.

Another salesperson was in an office where the manager, a significant person in his life, was under great pressure from the home office. Because of

THE SALES SLUMP DOCTOR IS IN!

this pressure, the manager was also in a slump and unable to provide this salesperson with the situational support and encouragement he needed. When I discovered this problem, I assumed the role and provided him with the necessary support and encouragement. He recovered from his slump with a sizable increase above his base month.

The female in the Experimental Group was unable to "crack" the market in which she chose to specialize. I discovered that she lacked the technical background to function in this market, and suggested that she meet with her manager to learn more about this market. The results were a rise from her Base Month of $1,393 to her Recovery Month of $5,345. She acquired the coping skills to function in her chosen market.

These techniques mentioned above come directly from Caplan's model as discussed earlier, and from my personal experience in selling.

Crisis intervention techniques can be taught to laypeople. In fact, most of the volunteers at crisis centers are laypeople and not professional psychologists. I believe, and the data indicates, that sales managers have a need to learn crisis intervention techniques to assist salespeople who are experiencing sales slumps.

This experiment concentrated on life insurance agents only, because sales records are intricately maintained, and, therefore, verifiable. However, I believe these results can be generalized to other sales organizations, and, further, to other groups subject to slumps.

The insurance industry, in particular, suffers from one of the highest attrition rates in the sales field. My own experience indicates that this is due to a philosophy in management that in order to maintain a sales force one must constantly recruit new agents, while little, if any, attention is paid to the existing agents after their initial training period. This is to ignore capital and constantly pursue income. Capital is the trained agent who usually receives too little attention too often, and who is allowed to slip out of the business when just a little attention would preserve this asset. When one looks at the tens of thousands of dollars invested in an agent over the first four years of his career it would appear self-evident that the insurance industry should undertake an immediate program aimed at agent conservation. The methods described in this study could form the basis for such a program. Of course, other sales fields also suffer from needless attrition, and, perhaps they too should examine how they deal with salespeople suffering from the age-old problem of the sales slump.

In the next chapter we shall explore the crisis model used in this experiment and learn how to use the balancing factors to restore salespeople to their previous level or higher level of selling.

CHAPTER 2

How the Mystery of Using Balancing Factors Got Me Out of My Slump.

Before we continue our dialog, let me take a few minutes to review what is meant by the term *crisis*. A crisis can occur when the normal state of balance comes under a stressful event that causes a loss of balance, and this state continues because of:

1. A distorted perception of the event causing the problem; and/or
2. No adequate situational support to overcome the problem; and/or
3. Inadequate coping mechanisms.

If any or all of these conditions remain unresolved, the loss of balance will continue and a crisis will develop. That's a mouthful, but if you will examine Figure 2.1, you can see what I mean.

Now I know you are wondering just what all this has to do with a slump, and how this information can help you overcome your next slump – but before I attempt to answer those questions, let me explain some of the terms in the description of crisis.

Remember in the preceding chapter when I made mention of feeling paranoid? Well, that was putting it mildly! If I called a prospect who did not want to see me, I was certain he hated me. You see, I truly developed a distorted perception of the events occurring to me, which worked to keep me in an unbalanced state that plunged me into a slump[6].

When I was not twisting reality into my own personal hell, I was looking to Sonia or my supervisor for some support in helping me out of my slump. Well, Sonia had her hands full with the girls (and, if the truth was known, really needed my support), and my supervisor had his own problems, leaving no time for me. I did not have adequate situational support. This, by itself, would be enough, but heaped atop my distortions of reality submerged me deeper and deeper into a slump.

To make matters worse, I did most of my business with people engaged in construction, and Savannah was experiencing one of its worst building depressions since the 1930s. But I did not know how to make my ideas attractive and applicable to prospects in other fields – I did not have adequate coping skills. Loss of balance continued. I plunged further and further into the slump!

FIGURE 2.1

CRISIS MODEL

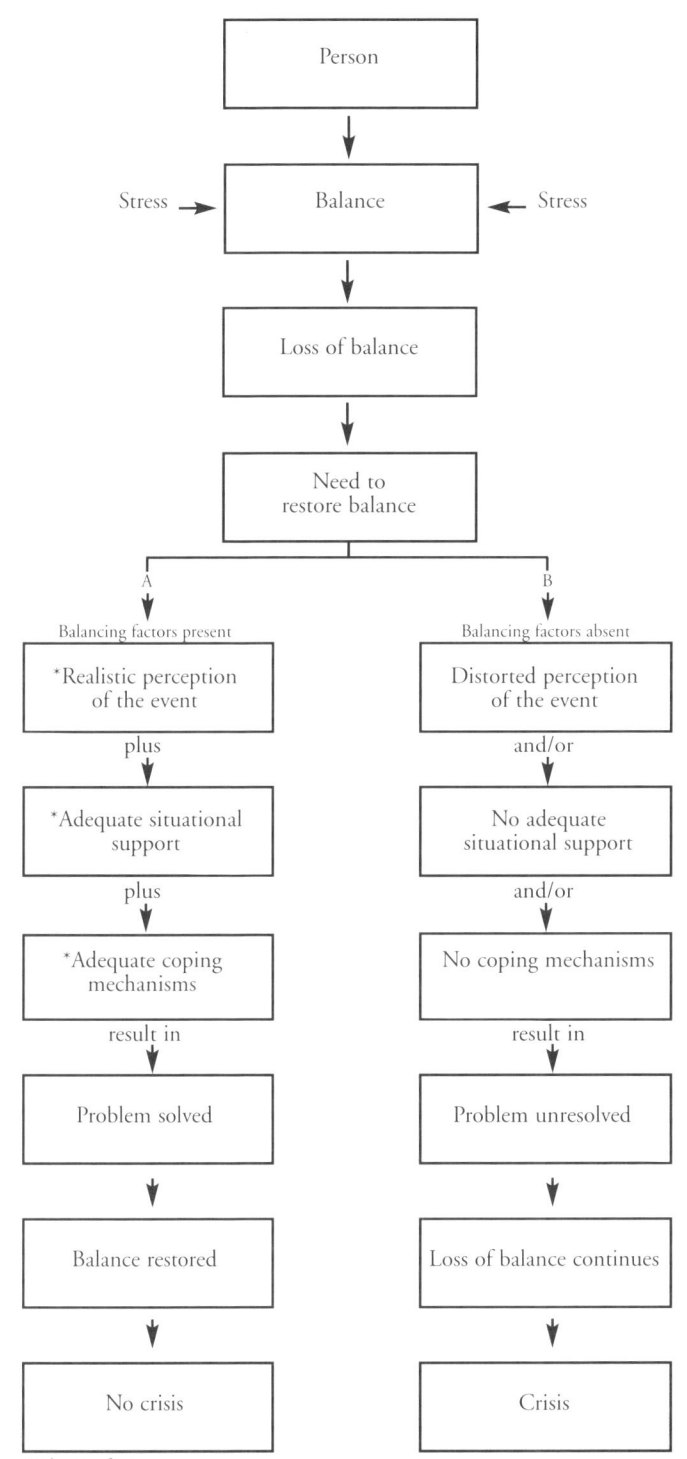

```
                    Person
                      ↓
    Stress →       Balance      ← Stress
                      ↓
                 Loss of balance
                      ↓
                    Need to
                 restore balance
              ↙                   ↘
              A                    B
   Balancing factors present   Balancing factors absent

   *Realistic perception       Distorted perception
        of the event               of the event
            plus                     and/or
            ↓                          ↓
   *Adequate situational         No adequate
        support                situational support
            plus                     and/or
            ↓                          ↓
   *Adequate coping            No coping mechanisms
     mechanisms
         result in                  result in
            ↓                          ↓
     Problem solved             Problem unresolved
            ↓                          ↓
    Balance restored         Loss of balance continues
            ↓                          ↓
       No crisis                      Crisis
```

*Balancing factors.

I entered the state of unbalance when I was unable to get appointments with what I thought were good prospects. I could not appropriately deal with the problem – usual methods failed! The problem persisted and intensified. Experiencing frustration, I rapidly exhausted my usual repertoire of coping skills. Emotional support from my environment vanished. Too late, I realized that my resources were inadequate; frustration and anxiety increased, and the stressful events became distorted. Without a solution, panic developed. I was now in an acute slump, feeling much distress and tension, desperately searching for help! Sounds bad? It was even worse.

Now let's look at a chart in the language of the salesperson. (Figure 2.2)

As you can see from the Anatomy of a Slump chart, the salesperson's state of balance is upset by external stress. This is in the form of lost sales or the inability to obtain appointments or an infinite number of other reasons. Some of these stressful situations occurred in the past without any effect on his normal balance; maybe all of these situations happened in the past without effecting this balance, but today – zap – he becomes unglued, "and all the king's horses and all the king's men couldn't put Humpty together again!"

Anxiety sets in, followed almost immediately by depression; loss of balance continues, and the need for balance gets stronger and stronger. Unsatisfied, this need causes frustration, which causes more anxiety, which causes more depression, which continues the loss of balance, which causes the need for balance to get stronger still, which causes more frustration, *ad nauseum!* Thank goodness this state is self-limiting.

Now the salesperson will attempt to restore balance to his world by working through one or more of the balancing factors. Failure at this point portends future failures whenever the situation is recreated.

You may have noticed in the Anatomy of a Slump chart that column A was left blank. This means that our salesperson had no balancing factors present. And success in treating the slump depends on a thorough understanding of these balancing factors. So let's begin with that, and look at the Anatomy of a Slump chart again – only this time we will fill in column A. (Figure 2.3)

Looking at column A, we will begin at the top – "Realistic perception of events." If, as in column B, you really believe your client hates you, then how can you get beyond this unrealistic perception of reality? How can you reach a correct conclusion using logic when your basic given (client hates me) is inherently defective? How? Try asking your supervisor, wife, significant other, etc. If there is someone close to your situation whom you trust, then that could be a good place to start, but get someone who can objectively analyze your personal situation and then offer suggestions.

FIGURE 2.2
ANATOMY OF A SLUMP

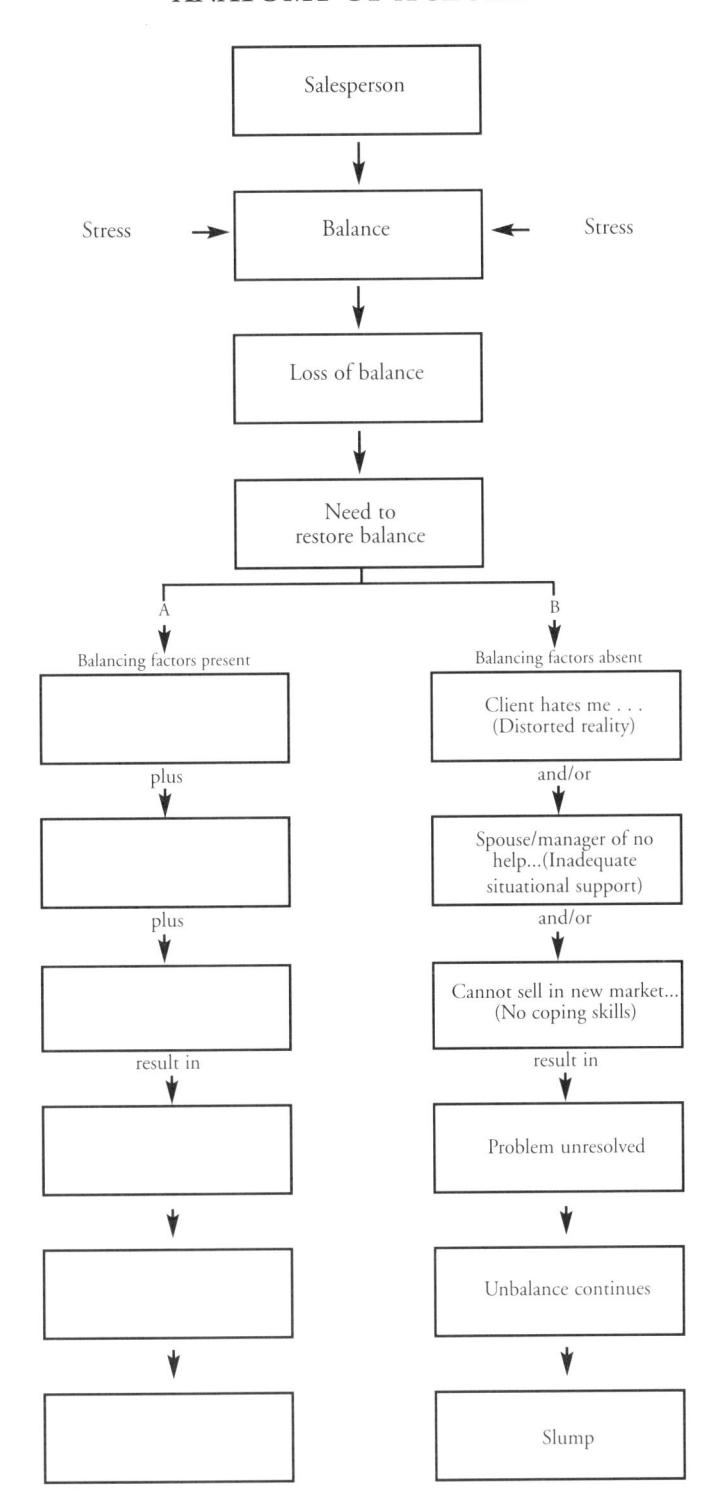

```
                    Salesperson
                         │
                         ▼
    Stress  →         Balance         ←  Stress
                         │
                         ▼
                   Loss of balance
                         │
                         ▼
                     Need to
                  restore balance
                   ┌─────┴─────┐
                   A           B
                   ▼           ▼
        Balancing factors   Balancing factors
            present             absent
                                  │
                                  ▼
        ┌─────────────┐    Client hates me . . .
        │             │    (Distorted reality)
        └─────────────┘
              plus            and/or
               ▼                ▼
        ┌─────────────┐   Spouse/manager of no
        │             │   help...(Inadequate
        └─────────────┘   situational support)
              plus            and/or
               ▼                ▼
        ┌─────────────┐   Cannot sell in new market...
        │             │   (No coping skills)
        └─────────────┘
            result in        result in
               ▼                ▼
        ┌─────────────┐   Problem unresolved
        │             │
        └─────────────┘
               ▼                ▼
        ┌─────────────┐   Unbalance continues
        │             │
        └─────────────┘
               ▼                ▼
        ┌─────────────┐       Slump
        │             │
        └─────────────┘
```

THE SALES SLUMP DOCTOR IS IN!

FIGURE 2.3

ANATOMY OF A SLUMP

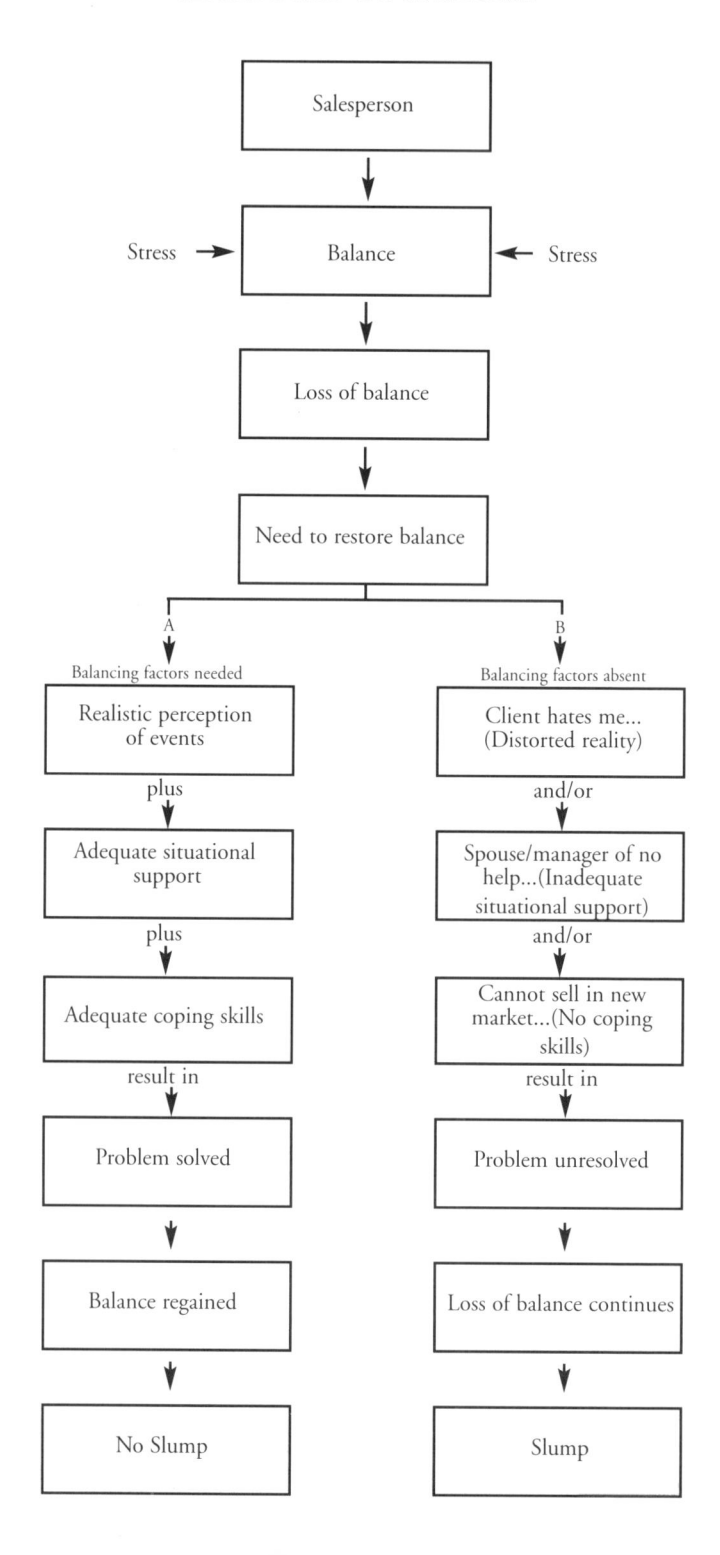

```
                        ┌─────────────┐
                        │ Salesperson │
                        └──────┬──────┘
                               ▼
          Stress  →     ┌─────────────┐     ←  Stress
                        │   Balance   │
                        └──────┬──────┘
                               ▼
                        ┌──────────────┐
                        │Loss of balance│
                        └──────┬───────┘
                               ▼
                     ┌──────────────────┐
                     │Need to restore   │
                     │    balance       │
                     └────┬─────────┬───┘
                        A │         │ B
                          ▼         ▼
         Balancing factors needed   Balancing factors absent
```

A — Balancing factors needed:
- Realistic perception of events
- *plus*
- Adequate situational support
- *plus*
- Adequate coping skills
- *result in*
- Problem solved
- ▼
- Balance regained
- ▼
- No Slump

B — Balancing factors absent:
- Client hates me...(Distorted reality)
- *and/or*
- Spouse/manager of no help...(Inadequate situational support)
- *and/or*
- Cannot sell in new market...(No coping skills)
- *result in*
- Problem unresolved
- ▼
- Loss of balance continues
- ▼
- Slump

THE SALES SLUMP DOCTOR IS IN!

One salesman I know developed an advisory board comprised of people who have utilized his services and who help him meet other people who could use his services. Whenever he has a new idea, he passes it by them to get their opinions, and whenever he encounters a problem he cannot resolve, he asks for their help. It works for him. It could work for you if you pick the right advisory board.

Situational support comes from those who are significant in your life. In other words, "Who loves you, baby?" This could be family or fellow workers or management, or again, that advisory board. Perhaps we need to discuss this in more detail.

As stated above, an advisory board is frequently composed of individuals who want to help you and who have something to bring to the table (knowledge, contacts, etc.). They can be people who utilize your services and who want to help, or they can be individuals who might never need your services. The one thing they must have in common is a willingness to help you in your chosen endeavors. How do you find such people? We will discuss this and all the other elements needed to form an advisory board in a later chapter.

We need to get back to the balancing factors and make certain you can muster the coping skills you will need when you need them. Well, just what are coping skills? They are the skills you need to successfully meet a given situation. In our example in the Anatomy of a Slump chart it would be the ability to sell in the new market. (Figure 2.4)

Treating the slump depends on a thorough understanding of the balancing factors shown in the crisis model on page 11. We already discussed the necessity of a realistic perception of events in order to maintain a state of equilibrium. A distorted perception of events leads to a slump. Earlier, the example of experiencing feelings of paranoia whenever a prospect would not give me an appointment was presented. No mention was made as to why I felt this way – only that I felt this way, and, how as a result, calling prospects for appointments came to a sudden halt. One reason might have been my distorted perception of the events (assuming, of course, the prospects really didn't hate me). But another could have been the result of not knowing how to get appointments in an unfamiliar market. This often results in a salesperson's distorted perception of the events as a direct result of inadequate coping skills. Then, before balance can be restored fully, you must teach the salesperson adequate coping skills *and* correct the distorted perception of events.

No, I'm not trying to change my tune by making something I previously said was relatively simple into something impossible. Remember, most crisis centers that deal successfully with crises are operated by volunteers who

THE SALES SLUMP DOCTOR IS IN!

FIGURE 2.4

ANATOMY OF A SLUMP

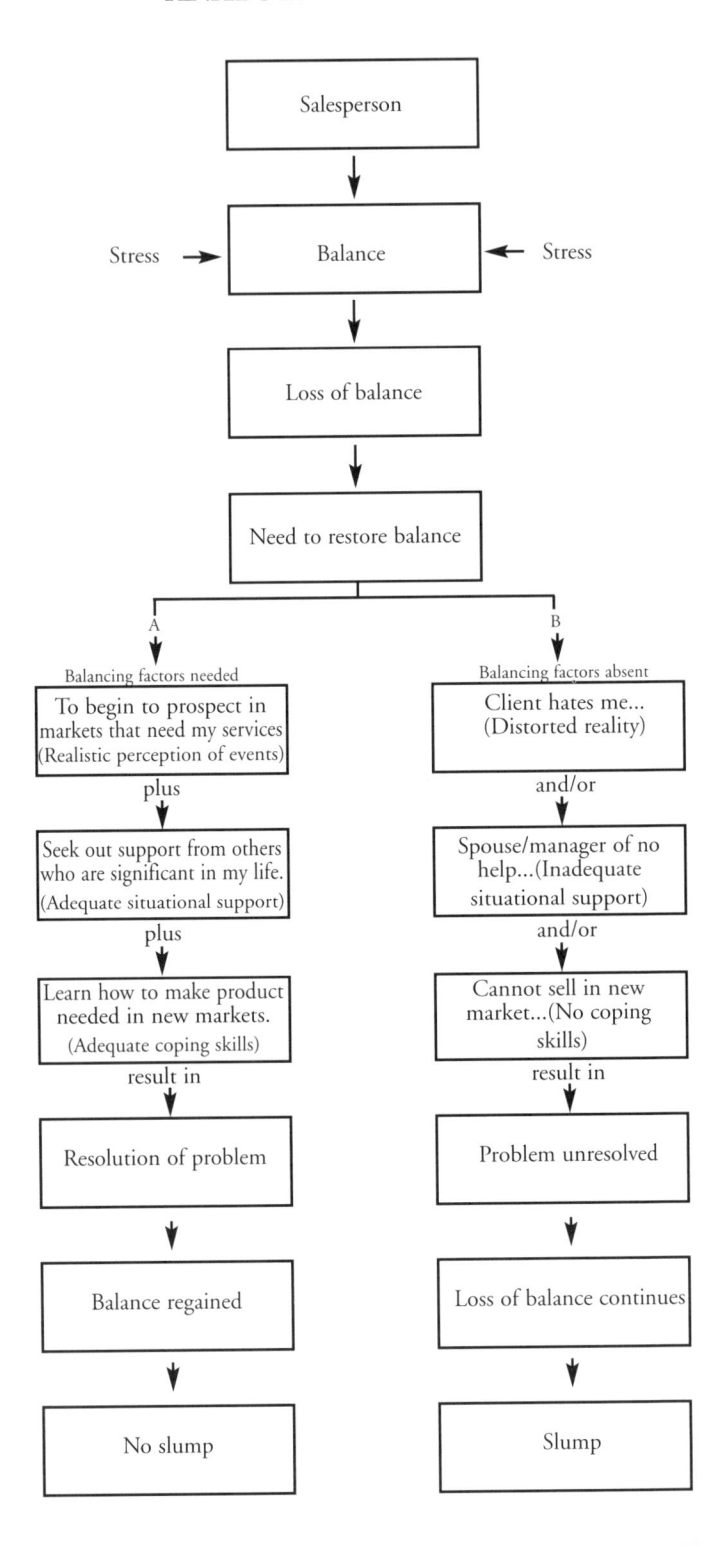

```
                    ┌─────────────┐
                    │ Salesperson │
                    └──────┬──────┘
                           ▼
         Stress →   ┌─────────────┐   ← Stress
                    │   Balance   │
                    └──────┬──────┘
                           ▼
                    ┌─────────────┐
                    │Loss of balance│
                    └──────┬──────┘
                           ▼
                    ┌──────────────────┐
                    │Need to restore balance│
                    └──────┬──────┬────┘
                           A      B
```

A — Balancing factors needed

- To begin to prospect in markets that need my services (Realistic perception of events)

  plus

- Seek out support from others who are significant in my life. (Adequate situational support)

  plus

- Learn how to make product needed in new markets. (Adequate coping skills)

  result in

- Resolution of problem
- Balance regained
- No slump

B — Balancing factors absent

- Client hates me...(Distorted reality)

  and/or

- Spouse/manager of no help...(Inadequate situational support)

  and/or

- Cannot sell in new market...(No coping skills)

  result in

- Problem unresolved
- Loss of balance continues
- Slump

THE SALES SLUMP DOCTOR IS IN!

have had limited training (usually twenty classroom hours followed by ten hours of on-the-job-training – similar to the programs we offer to salesmanagers). The point is this; you can help yourself and/or other salespeople out of slumps if you will invest a little time to learn and understand how to utilize the balancing factors.

The Chinese symbols for crisis are *wei-chi*. These symbols mean dangerous opportunity, and I would be hard-pressed to find a more appropriate description of a slump/crisis. So, if you are in a slump now, if you know someone who is, or the very next time you feel a slump coming on, remember these symbols. Know there is danger – you could utterly fail. Know there is opportunity – you could learn to succeed beyond your greatest expectations. Know there is help – seek it!

CHAPTER 3

You, Too, Can End Your Sales Slumps

As stated at the end of the previous chapter, "Treating the slump depends on a thorough understanding of the balancing factors shown in the CRISIS MODEL." That is why an entire section is devoted to this subject, and why it is placed early in our discussion.

BILL'S STORY

A while back, Bill, a life insurance salesman walked into my office. I took one look and immediately wondered, "Who died?" Fortunately, nothing that tragic had occurred. My friend was in the depths of the worst slump he ever experienced. His skin looked ashen, he had lost about fifteen pounds and his clothes hung on his body. His chin almost drooped into his lap. He couldn't make eye contact, and in a very low, frightened voice, he asked for help. He had spent the last twenty-four hours contemplating suicide. I said, "Bill, tell me about it," and tell me about it he did!

Bill had experienced a degree of success selling insurance, and instead of being the shoemaker who stuck to his last, he was convinced that success in one field *ipso facto* meant success in all fields. So, with the help of a friend who wanted to leave a civil service position, Bill became a builder — an instant builder. Initially, they built four houses under a low cost government-housing program. They sold immediately, and the world's newest builders were off to the races! The races, of course, meant running out and buying all the available lots they could with the bank's money to build more low cost government houses. As soon as the dynamic duo had secured far too many lots, the government withdrew their program. Bill's friend who talked him into the building business went to a resort area "to get a fresh start," and when Bill came to see me, the bank was about to foreclose.

Additionally, during this period that extended over several months, Bill stopped selling insurance to devote his efforts to the new venture. Unfortunately for him, the grass only *looked* greener. So, in addition to the bank being on his back, his creditors in general began asking questions about their money. By the time Bill came to me for help, he was at the lowest ebb of a full-blown slump, and most definitely in a state of disequilibrium.

It didn't take long to discover he was avoiding his bankers and creditors because "they are out to ruin me." After I hit him with some reality, he agreed to set up a meeting with his bankers and other creditors to propose a method of debt reduction that would keep them happy and leave him enough money each month to support his family. When he did this, he stopped fearing his creditors, and suddenly realized that they really needed to help him survive – if he survives, they get paid.

I also learned that neither Bill's wife nor his general agent was providing the situational support he needed to regain his balance. I asked Catherine to come in so that we could discuss Bill's problem. After letting her vent her frustrations and anger over the problem, I explained how important her support is to Bill, especially now. After she realized her role in getting him over his slump, she agreed to give Bill the support he needed.

Bill and I both realized he didn't have the necessary experience (coping skills) to close out the construction business. He decided to hire someone to finalize this chapter of his life.

Setting up the meeting with the creditors, getting Catherine back in Bill's corner, and the decision to hire an expert to close out the construction business were all that was needed to get Bill back to selling insurance – the thing he does best.

On the following page you will find the Anatomy of a Slump chart (Figure 3.1), and in the top rectangle you will find the name "Bill." Bill, as you know from the above history, was under a great deal of stress due to money problems and the fact that his erstwhile partner had skipped out on him (rectangle 2). Because of this, he lost his normal state of balance (rectangle 3) and felt the need to restore balance (rectangle 4).

Column A is where you can write in any balancing factors that are present, and column B is where you write in what is missing. I have filled in the blanks on this one to be used as a guide. All other charts in this chapter will be blank so you can practice your new skills!

What are these coping skills? How do we acquire them? What do they do? In the process of living we learn to use many problem-solving techniques to deal with anxiety and reduce tension. Our lifestyles develop around patterns of response which have been established to deal with stressful situations. These lifestyles are unique to us, and are very necessary to the maintenance of our natural equilibrium. Remember the first time a prospect said "No," and you didn't know how to go on from there? You bet you do! You felt the blood rush out of your face, your stomach tightened, your vocal cords froze, and you died right on the spot!

Somehow you got back to your office and your supervisor told you something like " . . . that wasn't really a 'No.' He was really saying you haven't given me enough information to earn the right to close." On the next appointment when you got to the point you expected to close, and once

THE SALES SLUMP DOCTOR IS IN!

FIGURE 3.1

ANATOMY OF A SLUMP

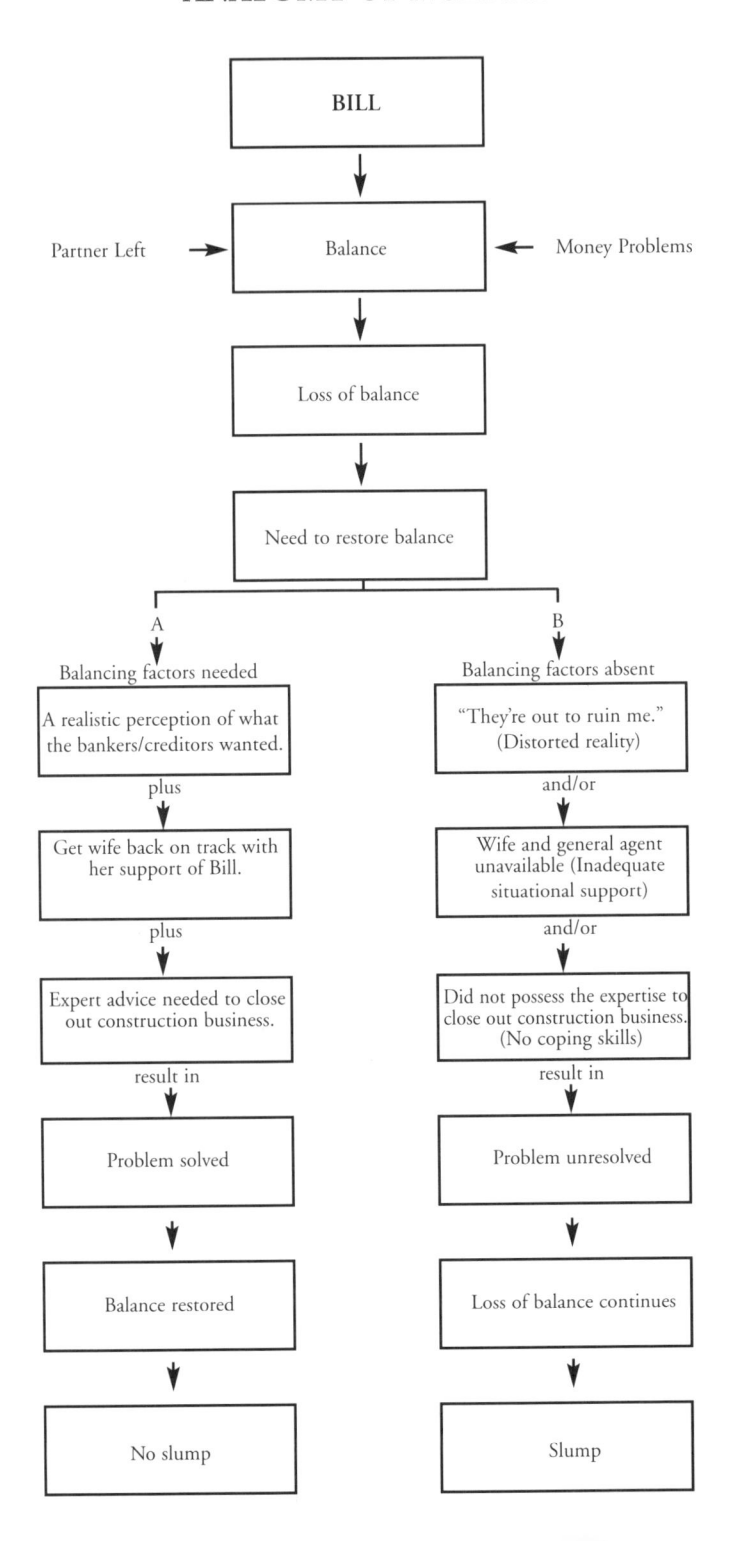

```
                            BILL
                             ↓
    Partner Left  →        Balance        ←  Money Problems
                             ↓
                       Loss of balance
                             ↓
                    Need to restore balance
                      ↓                ↓
                      A                B
          Balancing factors needed    Balancing factors absent

  A realistic perception of what    "They're out to ruin me."
  the bankers/creditors wanted.     (Distorted reality)
              plus                         and/or
              ↓                              ↓
  Get wife back on track with       Wife and general agent
  her support of Bill.              unavailable (Inadequate
                                    situational support)
              plus                         and/or
              ↓                              ↓
  Expert advice needed to close     Did not possess the expertise to
  out construction business.        close out construction business.
                                    (No coping skills)
           result in                       result in
              ↓                              ↓
         Problem solved              Problem unresolved
              ↓                              ↓
        Balance restored           Loss of balance continues
              ↓                              ↓
           No slump                        Slump
```

THE SALES SLUMP DOCTOR IS IN!

again you hear "No," only this time you didn't die – you said something like "... Mr. Prospect, let's go over this again so I can see what it is I didn't properly explain, etc.," and this time when you were ready for your next close he said "Yes!"

The first close netted you a "No" that caused stress to bombard your normal state of equilibrium. This caused anxiety and tension, which, if left uncorrected, leads to disequilibrium. You go straight to slump – you do not pass Go; you do not collect $200. When you change the unsuccessful close into an objection, or better yet, a question, you are responding to the challenge successfully – you learn to cope with the situation adequately, and, thus, you restore equilibrium and prevent a possible slump. This coping skill will be used over and over again in your selling whenever you encounter a similar stressful situation. Without this skill, in all probability you will die on the spot every time you get a "No," because you learned an inadequate coping skill that will keep you in slump after slump. The wise individual constantly evaluates his coping skills in all phases of his life.

KEN'S STORY

One day I met with Ken whose complaint was that he repeatedly goes through slump, after slump, after slump. He asked, "Doctor, what can I do to prevent these recurring slumps? It seems that I go along successfully for a short period and then another slump. What can I do?"

We discussed his work habits, years of experience, etc., and then I reviewed the Slump Intervention Model with him. I told him there were three questions he could ask himself:

1. Is my perception of reality, as it applies to this slump, correct?
2. Do I have the support from others that I need?
3. Do I have the required coping skills?

Unless the answer to all three questions is yes, you will remain in an unbalanced state with all of the accompanying discomforts and proceed directly to a slump. Knowing this and doing this can be worlds apart. Many of us do not have that very special mirror that allows us to see our environment and ourselves as they really are. Sometimes we make it too pretty and other times too ugly to be real. Someone once told me that trying to see one's self objectively is like trying to see the back of your head with a single mirror.

When Ken first came to me he was suffering an identity crisis that plunged him into a devastating slump. It manifested itself by disabling his ability to sell.

Ken had been married for several years and was the father of two teenage sons who were honor students. His wife was active in community organizations. They had a lovely home in one of the city's most prestigious areas, and they were sought-after socially. Aside from Ken's identity crisis, they were the ideal family.

What I did was help him view his crisis and discuss how it related to his slump. Ken viewed things in the extreme. They were either all black or all white. Gray did not exist. It seemed that the rather comfortable world he built over the years and the world he now wanted to construct were in conflict. Viewing the world as he did left his thoughts scrambled. He felt he wasn't doing anything constructive for his fellow man by just selling, and if he wanted to help his fellow man he had to quit selling, which he could not do because his lifestyle required money. He felt his goals had all been for naught, and that his first 40 years of life were a complete waste. What he now wanted was some form of spiritual satisfaction that his present world was not providing. After all, the world doesn't produce a surplus of Mother Theresas.

He had to be helped to realign his view of reality so he could correctly see he was not doing anything that needed to be discontinued in order to enjoy a more spiritual life. And, as a matter of fact, he had to continue doing all that he was doing so he could meet his obligations to his family and creditors. He finally decided to accept a role of leadership in his religious affiliation to help him fulfill his inner hunger to do more for his fellow man. Actually, this new venture not only gave him the satisfaction he so badly craved, but it increased his personal income by nearly $35,000 the first year, and has grown each year since. I guess you really can serve yourself best when you choose to serve others.

Now it's your turn. On the next page is Ken's Anatomy of a Slump chart. (Figure 3.2) If you are not clear about the facts or the balancing factors, re-read Ken's story and then fill out the chart. You can get the answers to this and other problems in Appendix A at the back of the book.

Let's look at some other cases presented to me by general agents and managers. This time we will use the following three steps to help these salespeople overcome their slumps. These are the exact steps used in the charts. To help you graphically view this process you can see these cases in chart form in Appendix A.

1. Is their perception of reality correct?
2. Do they have the support from others that is needed?
3. Do they have the required coping skills?

FIGURE 3.2

ANATOMY OF A SLUMP

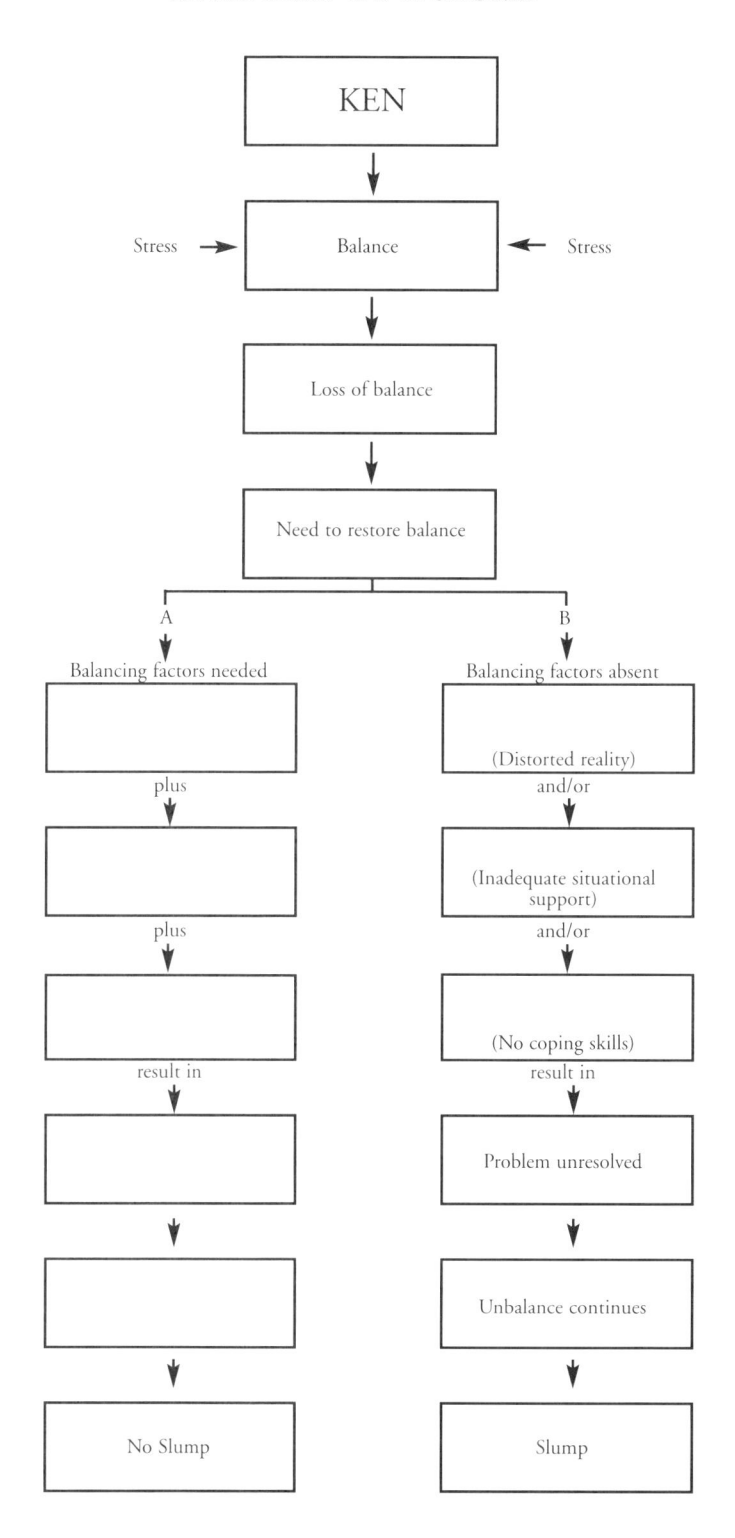

```
                        ┌──────────────┐
                        │     KEN      │
                        └──────┬───────┘
                               ↓
          ┌────────────────────────────────────┐
Stress → │              Balance                │ ← Stress
          └────────────────┬───────────────────┘
                           ↓
                  ┌──────────────────┐
                  │  Loss of balance │
                  └────────┬─────────┘
                           ↓
                ┌──────────────────────┐
                │ Need to restore balance │
                └──────┬────────┬──────┘
                       A        B
```

A	B
Balancing factors needed	Balancing factors absent
	(Distorted reality)
plus	and/or
	(Inadequate situational support)
plus	and/or
	(No coping skills)
result in	result in
	Problem unresolved
↓	↓
	Unbalance continues
↓	↓
No Slump	Slump

CASE STUDY 1:

Doug had been in sales for a number of years before he was hired as a life insurance agent. His previous company was going through some changes and he felt that he would be out of a job if he hung around. His general agent told me that "during the interview process, he seemed like a good people person, but now that he was on my payroll, he couldn't seem to close any sales." He had lots of sales calls, and lots of open cases, but no final results, which equated to no money for him. His wife was now concerned that maybe this was not the field that he should be in and Doug was beginning to wonder if he had made the wrong decision in coming into the life insurance industry.

When Doug and his general agent came to me to discuss his progress, it was evident that Doug was feeling pretty low. He spoke in whispers without making eye contact, and was on the verge of tears. When he finally opened up he said things at home were rough. His wife was constantly on his case about not having enough money and about all the evenings he had to work late seeing prospects. Now, he wondered if he had made a wrong decision. He had never failed in a job before. He always left for a better opportunity. He was concerned. No money was coming in and his wife was putting pressure on him to start looking for another job. She was scared and so was he.

I asked him to go over his last few interviews and tell me exactly what had occurred. It was obvious that Doug followed the sales process, but he never asked the prospect to buy. When I asked him why he did not ask them to buy, his reply was, "If they didn't say 'no' I didn't have to throw that prospect card away and look for someone else." With some coaching and support, and with his general agent going on some joint appointments with him, he was able to start asking his prospects for their business and started closing sales. His confidence increased and so did his bank account. He was back on track and all was well at home.

QUESTION:

Using the steps to get out of a slump, what did the general agent and I do? The answer is shown below, but try to solve the problem before looking at the answer.

Do not forget to answer these three questions before reading the answer.
1. Is his perception of reality as it applies to the slump correct?
2. Does he have the support from others that he needs?
3. Does he have the required coping skills to solve his problems?

THE SALES SLUMP DOCTOR IS IN!

ANSWER:

When checking whether he was correctly dealing with his idea of reality, we discovered that Doug had the wrong concept of what a prospect card was. It wasn't something to hoard. It was only good if you could qualify it and then close it. If you couldn't do that you had to get rid of it. Doug accepted this and corrected his concept of reality.

Secondly, Doug wasn't getting situational support from his wife due to her fears. His general agent provided the necessary situational support by showing his sincere concern for Doug's welfare. Of course, when Doug's slump ended, his wife's fears also vanished.

Finally, the general agent showed Doug how to ask for the money, and this provided him with the necessary coping skills.

CASE STUDY 2:

Matt had other problems. He was an ex-Marine sergeant who was used to being in charge. He had a very confident exterior, but that proved to be false. He breezed through all of the pre-contract work required of him and had an impressive prospect list. He presented great plans for really getting a flying start in this business. Once he went through all of his friends and family, people who knew he was an ex-Marine sergeant, things came to a screeching halt. He just dried up and stopped calling anyone – including the referrals that he had obtained from friends and family. He kept busy by just moving papers around and was constantly just getting ready to get ready!

His general agent saw what was happening and realized that they had a problem here. The three of us sat down together and talked about his activity and the lack of any follow through with new prospects. After all the excuses, we finally got to the bottom line. He froze when it came to calling on strangers. All those years of playing the role of the tough Marine were just that, a role. Now he was afraid to make calls if he didn't personally know the prospects. He couldn't tell his wife, but she was beginning to wonder why he wasn't progressing in his work, and she was losing patience because of the lack of income.

QUESTION:

Using the same steps mentioned in Case Study 1, what would you do?

ANSWER:

Matt thought he had to be on near intimate terms with someone before he could ask for an appointment, and his wife was doing anything but giving him the support he needed to overcome his slump and stick with the business. He was also unwilling to learn to use new techniques to improve his coping skills. Therefore, he became an ex-agent.

AFTER THOUGHT:

Don't look at this as a failure. A long time ago I learned that I couldn't dance with all the pretty girls. Some just didn't want to dance with me. This is true with helping others when they are in slumps . . . I just cannot help everyone. At first I viewed situations like this as complete failure. What a distorted perception of reality! Since when did success hinge on 100% winning? In short, it doesn't.

After I got my head straight I was able to accept the fact that everyone is not savable, just as everyone is not a prospect – you eliminate and move on. Sometimes a hard lesson for new sales managers to learn.

CASE STUDY 3:

Frank, a successful life insurance agent, spent 17 years working as an agent in a general agency where he was regarded as a role model. During this period he always had a general agent, peers, and generally enjoyed a great deal of support and respect from his environment. He decided it was time to strike out on his own and become a personal producing general agent. His production was such that he could easily afford to assume the new expenses – the gamble he was taking for the added commissions. Things proceeded as he hoped, and production was booming.

Meanwhile, his children grew to the point where his wife was free to consider the life-long dream of becoming a nurse. After some family discussion, she enrolled in nursing school with everyone's blessing.

One would think that things couldn't be better. Upon closer examination you could see that Frank was no longer anyone's role model; he no longer had his general agent and peers for support, and now he lost his wife's support due to her study demands. He said he felt as though he had been set adrift and his sales were suffering. Not only did he have the drop in income, but he had also taken on new financial obligations in the form of operating his own office. He wanted help.

QUESTION:

What would you advise Frank to do?

ANSWER:

Frank was advised to develop a support group of other personal producing general agents.[7] This turned out to be a wonderful self-help support group where they provided situational support, among other things, for each other. He did this and overcame his slump.

THE SALES SLUMP DOCTOR IS IN!

After reviewing the proceeding, it is easy to see that Frank had trouble obtaining the situational support he needed. It was easy for me, a professional, to see this, but will you be able to do this? How will you get the information you need? Where will you begin? In the next chapter I will offer some comments and direction on obtaining the information needed to help.

CHAPTER 4

How Do You Get Them To Talk? You Listen, Listen, Listen!
This Also Works Like Magic in Sales Interviews

After reading the previous chapters you might be asking how do you get the necessary information to help the salesperson in a sales slump? Let us explore some of the avenues you will use.

ATTENDING SKILLS

When communicating with someone it is important to let them know we are listening. Attending to the person is the first step in establishing a relationship. If the salesmanager is relaxed he is already beginning to attend. Being relaxed and having concern in your voice communicate, "I am ready to listen." There are specific behaviors that further communicate attention. They are classified as non-verbal or verbal.

Some non-verbal attending behaviors are:
1. Relaxed Posture
2. Eye Contact
3. Nodding Your Head
4. Facial Expression

Some verbal attending behaviors are:
1. Voice Tone
2. Minimal Encouragements:
    a. One Word Statements
    b. Following Comments

In face-to-face contact both verbal and non-verbal cues can be used to let the other person know you are listening. (The reason I stress face-to-face contact is because in today's business world you might well be communicating over the phone or some other electronic means of communication. This type of communication is not your everyday face-to-face contact.) Of all the non-verbal cues, eye contact, in my opinion, is the most important. Looking at a person while he talks to you communicates attention. None or limited eye contact communicates inattention, boredom, restlessness, uneasiness, etc. Eye contact should be maintained as frequently as practical in face-to-face contacts. Nodding your head or smiling (if appropriate) further communicate attention. These non-verbal behaviors used in an atmosphere of relaxation communicate a high level of attention.

THE SALES SLUMP DOCTOR IS IN!

Can you remember trying to speak to someone and having them shuffle papers or look for something on their desk? You know darn well they are not particularly interested in what you have to say. Remember this whenever you are communicating with another person.

Verbal attending cues are voice tone plus minimal encouragements. The verbal cue immediately perceived is voice tone, and whether it sounds relaxed and caring. To communicate, "I am listening," the voice tone needs to be calm and concerned. Minimal encouragements are brief verbal comments which indicate to the salesperson that the salesmanager is listening and it is OK to continue talking. There are two basic forms of minimal encouragements. One form consists of one or two word comments ("Uh-huh," "Mn," "Yes," "Go on," "And," and so forth) used at appropriate pauses in the salesperson's dialogue. Following comments is the other form. These must be relevant to what the salesperson stated. Following comments are often reflections or repetitions of a word or two of what was just said. For example:

1. "That prospect really upset me!"   Salesmanager: "Upset you?"
                                                      "Prospect?"
2. "I really feel great!"   "Great?"

The message communicated here is, "Go ahead," "I'm listening," "Tell me more." These verbal cues effectively relate to the salesperson that you are listening and concerned. This aids in the formation of the relationship.

When meeting face-to-face verbal and non-verbal cues are used to communicate attention. As stated earlier, when in phone contact non-verbal skills cannot be used. Therefore, verbal attending behaviors become critical and must be used to compensate for this loss. Silence on the phone can communicate to the salesperson that his salesmanager is busy doing something else or is not even there. Needless to say, this must be avoided. Minimal encouragement at appropriate pauses will let the salesperson know you are there and listening. Increased verbal following will also help. Caution: too frequent use of verbal cues will have a negative effect. It might communicate inattention or indifference. You must discover your appropriate level of responding and use it.

RELATIONSHIP OF LISTENING SKILLS TO SLUMP INTERVENTION STAGES

The use of attending skills help work through the slump intervention stages of emotional contact and clarification. As the salesmanager attends the salesperson, the salesperson experiences a feeling of relief that someone is concerned and willing to listen. Emotional contact is made. Attending behaviors keep a salesperson talking and the more he talks the greater the ease and likelihood of their gaining clarification. One of my old gurus, the late Dr. Milton Erickson, was famous for saying, "If you let the patient talk long enough he will tell you how to cure him." The same is true here.

OPEN-ENDED QUESTIONS

When you initially make contact with the salesperson in a sales slump it is necessary to acquire certain information and some questions will be needed. Generally, two broad classes of questions are used – closed questions and open questions. Closed questions elicit specific information. They provide a definite structure and limit the salesperson's choices of responses. With closed questions, the salesmanager remains in control providing direction while the salesperson passively supplies answers. Contrary to this, open-ended questions elicit broad areas of information. Little structure is provided and control is passed over to the salesperson so that he may respond as he sees fit. Examples of open-ended and closed questions are:

CLOSED QUESTIONS	OPEN-ENDED QUESTIONS
How old are you?	
Where do you live?	Would you tell me about yourself?
Are you married?	
Where do you work?	
What do you do?	Could you tell me about your work?
How do you like your work?	

Whenever possible open-ended questions should be used in slump intervention interviews. These questions provide more information, give responsibility for direction to the salesperson, and are more efficient than closed questions. Minimal urging following open-ended questions keeps the salesperson talking, which provides more information. However, minimal urging following closed questions usually runs into a dead-end – the person questioned frequently has nothing more to say. Closed questions can be used following open-ended questions to clarify the information obtained.

RELATIONSHIP OF COMMUNICATION SKILLS TO SLUMP INTERVENTION STAGES

Open-ended questions assist in working through the stages of **clarification, mobilization,** and **goal setting.** Open-ended questions allow the salesperson to discuss what he needs to discuss, and as he talks, he gains **clar-**

THE SALES SLUMP DOCTOR IS IN!

ification or gives the salesmanager information to use for **clarification.** Open-ended questions can provide information about immediate resources and, as a result, lead to **mobilization.** Likewise, they can elicit information about existing coping behavior and desired goals. This can lead to the formulation of a plan of action.

LEVELS OF LISTENING AND RESPONDING

LEVEL 1: THE UNRELATED RESPONSE

The unrelated response is one that introduces a subject that is completely different from the one initiated by the first speaker.

>   Example: **Speaker 1:** I lost a big sale yesterday, but fortunately I can still meet my quota.
>   **Speaker 2:** Have you heard that the Jaguars are trading Mark Brunell?

LEVEL 2: THE TANGENTIAL RESPONSE

The tangential response is one which picks up on a word or thought contained in the statement of the first speaker, but which directs the discussion away from the purpose of the first speaker.

>   Example: **Speaker 1:** I lost a big sale yesterday, but fortunately I can still meet my quota.
>   **Speaker 2:** I heard that Neiman Marcus is having a big sale. Maybe we should get there early to see if we can pick up some bargains.

LEVEL 3: THE FURTHERING RESPONSE

The furthering response is one which, either verbally or non-verbally, encourages the first speaker to continue on with what he was saying.

>   Example: **Speaker 1:** I lost a big sale yesterday, but fortunately I can still meet my quota.
>   **Speaker 2:** Was it the buy-sell deal at the ABC Company?

LEVEL 4: THE FEELING RESPONSE

The feeling response is one that focuses in on the feeling expressed or implied in the statement of the first speaker. Frequently, the second speaker will respond by also expressing their own feeling while acknowledging the feeling of the other.

Example: **Speaker 1:** I lost a big sale yesterday, but fortunately I can still meet my quota.
Speaker 2: I can understand why you are relieved that you can meet your quota.

There are several general statements that can be made relating to the levels of response. First, **Level 1** and **Level 2** responses shift the focus of response from the first speaker to the second speaker. They are self-oriented responses that take the ball away from the first speaker. **Level 3** and **Level 4** responses allow **Speaker 1** to maintain the focus and is encouraged to continue with his original point. His feelings are also acknowledged and often accepted.

Level 3 responses frequently take the form of questions and seek additional information from **Speaker 1** on the subject he initiated.

Level 4 responses are always furthering. They refer directly to the feelings of **Speaker 1** and keep the focus on him.

There is an implied value judgment in the four levels. **Levels 3 and 4** responses are better than **Levels 1** and **2**. However, there can be many instances when it is desirable to shift the focus away from the speaker – especially if they have been monopolizing the discussion. What is important is that you be aware of the nature of the salesperson's response and use the **Level 1** and **2** responses when appropriate.

LISTENING FOR FEELINGS

When you listen for feelings you not only hear what is being said, but also what is not being said. You hear the emotion behind the words. Haven't you heard someone saying they apologize for something they did, and all the while they are chuckling under their breath? What are they really saying? Certainly not that they are sincerely sorry for what they did.

TWELVE WAYS TO REALLY SCREW UP ANY RAPPORT YOU MIGHT HAVE DEVELOPED WITH YOUR SALESPEOPLE WHEN YOU ARE TRYING TO GET THEM TO "DO THEIR JOB."

(THIS SECTION IS ALSO KNOWN AS "ROADBLOCKS TO COMMUNICATIONS.")

Suppose your salesperson is having a difficult time meeting higher sales quota. Somehow he lets the salesmanager know about this problem and that it is really bothering him. Here are some typical responses from the salesmanager that close all avenues of communication:

THE SALES SLUMP DOCTOR IS IN!

1. *Ordering or commanding* – example – "Stop complaining and get your work done."
2. *Warning or threatening* – example – "You better shape up if you want to keep your job."
3. *Moralizing, preaching, giving "shoulds" and "oughts"* – example – "You know it's your job to sell the product." "You should leave your personal problems at home where they belong."
4. *Advising or offering solutions* – example – "The thing for you to do is to start working earlier." "Then you'll have more time for selling."
5. *Teaching, lecturing, giving logical arguments* – example – "Let's look at the facts." "You only have 15 more days to make your quota."

The above examples offer solutions to the salesperson. The next three examples communicate judgment, evaluation or put-downs.

6. *Judging, criticizing, disagreeing, blaming* – example – "You're either a complete goof-off or an accomplished procrastinator."
7. *Name-calling, stereotyping, labeling* – example – "You're acting like an adolescent, not like a pro representing this company."
8. *Interpreting, analyzing, diagnosing* – example – "What do you mean they won't give you appointments?" "You must be paranoid."

The next two messages are attempts by the salesmanager to make the salesperson feel better – to make the problem go away – or to deny that a problem exists.

9. *Praising, agreeing, giving positive evaluations* – example – "You're one heck of a salesperson." "I'm sure you'll figure out how to meet your quota."
10. *Reassuring, sympathizing, consoling, supporting* – example – "You're not alone when it comes to having a bad month." "I've experienced tough months, too." "Besides, when you start making sales again you'll roll right past your quota."

The next one is the most frequently used roadblock even though salesmanagers realize that questions often produce defensiveness. Also, questions are most often used when the salesmanager feels he needs more facts because he plans to solve the salesperson's problem by presenting the best of all possible solutions, rather than help the salesperson solve their own problem. (Give a person a fish and you feed him for a day. Teach a person to fish and you feed him for life.)

11. *Questioning, probing, interrogating, cross-examining* – example – "Do you think your quota is too high?" "How much time have you spent on it?" "Why did you wait so long to come to me?"

This last category consists of methods that salesmanagers use to change the subject, divert the salesperson, or avoid having to deal with the salesperson at all.

12. *Withdrawing, distracting, being sarcastic, humoring, diverting* – example – "Ah come on, can't we talk about something more pleasant?" "This is a bad time?" "Let's get back to making calls." "Seems like someone has a burr under their saddle today."

All of the dirty dozen tell the salesperson that you are non-accepting of their problem. This will stop any dialog in its tracks. Remember, the name of this article is *How Do You Get Them To Talk? You Listen, Listen Listen!* But you also have to know how to listen. If you don't know what this means, go directly back to the beginning and re-read!

(NOTE: I consider communication skills to be the key to utilizing Slump Intervention Techniques – so much so that I have added a Bonus Workbook to this book that is a training manual designed to teach trainers how to teach communication skills. The reader will also benefit from practicing the skills presented in this manual. I hope you find it useful.)

CHAPTER 5

How Forming Your Own Board of Directors Will Solve Your Prospecting Woes
or, The Lord Helps Those Who Help Themselves!

Don't you just love clichés. They sound full and meaningful, but they just don't tell us how. It would have been nice if they came with owner manuals. That way with each cliché we would be able to know just how to apply it to our life-situation.

What most salespeople really want to know is, "What can I do to keep my production steady and growing?" And to do that they need to ask, "How can I find enough prospects to make my planned quota for this period?" That, my friend, appears to be universal to every salesperson. It must be mastered if you want to make it in selling.

The best way I know to stay on target is through a system of record keeping. Let me tell you about a life insurance agent who was puzzled by what was happening to him when he came to me for help. He had a goal of making two sales a week for 50 weeks per year. He knew it took him an average of 20 calls to get four appointments to make one sale. To reach his weekly goal required 40 calls to obtain 8 appointments to make 2 sales. He had done this for years, but now he was in a slump. He was making his calls, but he could not get appointments. No appointments meant no sales!

After some discussion, I asked him to go into the other office and call me for an appointment. At first he thought I was kidding, but after some assurance that I was not, he went into the other office and called me for an appointment. Unknown to him, I taped his call.

I was the typical prospect – polite, but cool. He told me all about his company and why I should own more insurance, but he never once asked me for an appointment. Instead, he was trying to sell me insurance over the phone. I finally ended the call and asked him to come back to my office.

When he returned I played the tape for him. When it was over, I asked him to tell me what he did wrong. Much to my surprise, he immediately said "I never asked for an appointment." He was correct. He learned a valuable lesson – when you call for an appointment you are closing only to get the appointment. Do not fall into the trap of trying to close the sale on the phone. It is too easy for the prospect to say "no" over the phone!

History is a wonderful teacher – especially our own history. If you listened carefully when you were learning the craft of selling you were told all about keeping records. And if you were dumb enough to do what the experts said would work, then you should have a ream of records of your selling history. So, if you know how many calls it takes to get an appointment and how many appointments it takes to earn the right to close and how many closes it takes to get a sale, then you will immediately know something is wrong if you are doing all the proper steps without getting the proper results. You may not know what to do about it, but you will know enough to know you are in trouble and to seek help. And salesmanagers get paid to provide just such help. Go to yours immediately!

If you are not keeping records of your calls-to-closes-to-sales ratios, I strongly recommend you do so. When I was first in the business, my home office provided me with a Weekly Planner that tracked all this for me. All I had to do was fill in the blanks. How's that for a no-brainer way of establishing these important ratios? "Just do it!"

One day I was having coffee with my banker and he told me he had to hurry because he had to go to a board meeting at the bank. Being inquisitive (nosey) I asked what they did at these meetings. His response led me to form a self-help group of colleagues. We met regularly to discuss new ideas and mutual problems. This was very helpful because its uses are as limitless as your imagination. What are some of the ways such a group could help you today?

If you want to form such a group here are some points to keep in mind:

- Have only one representative from each professional group, such as an attorney, CPA, casualty insurance agent, real estate agent, banker, different type of sales agent, etc.
- Meet only once a month – breakfast or lunch usually work best.
- Have stated purposes such as exchange of referrals, brainstorming new tax codes or products for ideas, learn how to use crisis intervention to help each other when in sales slumps, review articles from trade magazines such as *Financial Services Advisor,* and so on. The group can dictate its purpose and can, as needed or desired, change the purpose.
- If a member misses two meetings in a row without ample reason, he is out.

"But how do you find the people to form the initial group?" is the question I frequently hear. I suggest that you set a date for a definite meeting and invite your close associates. Fully explain the purpose of the meeting when you issue the invitation and be certain to ask each invitee to bring an associate who could benefit from the group. If you get five people to come

THE SALES SLUMP DOCTOR IS IN! 37

and they each bring someone with them who is interested in forming such a group, then you will have 11 group members including yourself. Give it a whirl – you have everything to gain.

Now that you've got the group, what do you do with it? As mentioned earlier, finding enough prospects to make your planned quota for each sales period is an ongoing problem. We all need other people, but the salesperson especially needs other people. So how can your board members help each other with this?

You each agree to share names with each other. How do you do this? Well, your board is composed of at least ten people other than yourself. Each of you brings in five qualified names to be given to every other member at each meeting. These are beautiful numbers – you will leave the meeting with fifty names of qualified prospects after each monthly meeting. My goodness, that's six hundred names a year! How's that for the time you took to form this group? And that's just the tip of the iceberg. Use your imagination; it's a gift from God.

Let me emphasize, if a person misses two meetings in a row without a very good excuse, they are out, and you invite another professional of the same background to join your group. You cannot afford to carry dead weight. That person cost you and every other member five names per meeting he misses.

All the members will, from time to time, have the opportunity to help and to be helped with problems or questions they bring to the floor. If the group initially does not have the experience to run itself, bring in a professional to get it started. If the group gets stuck – bring the professional back until the group can refocus and move on. As the group matures, older members will drop out and newer members will join. This is healthy and tends to rejuvenate the group.

If you feel yourself slipping below your norm, ask for help. Wow, that's a simple statement, but you cannot imagine how hard it is for me to get others to do just that – ask for help. You can explain your need for help to those close to you and especially your supervisor. Ask them to periodically meet with you to help when your battery is low. Let them know their role in keeping you balanced. This is a good idea because those close to you frequently notice subtle changes long before they become problematic, and certainly long before you become aware of them. When you ask for help your job is to listen, listen, listen.

The life insurance industry offers inservice study courses such as L.U.T.C. and C.L.U. that will keep your coping skills, etc., current. Companies offer similar, but usually more basic, services. The M.D.R.T. spends much of its budget dispensing new ideas and technical skills to its members to help them cope with an ever-changing marketplace. Just about every field in selling has its own sources of new ideas and new technical changes that are constantly available to help the salesperson cope. Use this material – your competitor will!

Incidentally, L.U.T.C. and C.L.U. classes frequently make excellent self-help groups. Usually, the members are from various companies and backgrounds, and the group benefits from these differences. Remember, if both of you think alike, one of you is not necessary! Of course, you cannot expect the sharing of prospects in such a group!

Finally, if you cannot find the help you need from any of the above mentioned areas, seek professional help. Not every psychologist or counselor will be able to help. They may lack the experience or interest in this area. Shop around and ask if they have had experience with your particular type of problem. If you get non-direct answers to your direct questions, keep on shopping. If all else fails, call me.

We have weekend crash workshops where we meet with salespeople from around the country and do marathon intervention groups. For those who require individual attention, individual slump intervention is available.

We also provide training in slump intervention techniques for salesmanagers, supervisors, salespeople, and others who can directly benefit from our work. Usually, their companies have me come in for a one or two day workshop.

Stop right now and list all of your slump prevention resources. The following brief questionnaire will help you compose your list.

THE SALES SLUMP DOCTOR IS IN!

SLUMP PREVENTION QUESTIONNAIRE

1. Where are my records, and are they current?

2. List three or more colleagues who have agreed to be part of my self-help group, and who have agreed to help me if I need them to do so.

   Name   Company Affiliation   Phone

3. Who helped during my last slump?

4. What did I do then that I am not doing now? Explain in detail.

CHAPTER 6

PAIN
THE GREATEST GIFT GOD GAVE SALES MANAGERS

"I'm going to kill myself."

I asked him, "Why?"

"Business has been awful," he said, "and my wife is going to take the kids and divorce me."

"What brought all this on," I asked.

"One heck of a slump," was his reply.

We talked. He cried. I tried to console him, but he didn't want consolation – He wanted help! The pain was more than he could bear.

Wow! What a golden opportunity. Imagine your salesman walking into your office and literally begging for help. He is willing to do anything to relieve the pain. Will you be able to seize the moment?

A LOOK AT SOME OPPORTUNITIES

Tony was a big spender. He earned big dollars and knew how to live. He had great confidence in his ability to continue doing this and didn't save for that rainy day. In fact, he was heavily in debt. Then something unexpected happened and Tony's life began a very rapid downward spiral. His oldest daughter, then sixteen, became pregnant, and he and his wife were at a loss as to what to do. He was a staunch pro-lifer and a former alter boy. She professed being a pro-lifer, but, now that it had hit home, she was teetering back and forth. He finally prevailed, and they decided to keep the daughter at home and then to raise the child as one of their own. No, they were not going to pretend that it was the wife's child. They felt that the best way to handle this was out in the open – especially in today's more understanding climate.

Tony was embarrassed by what had happened and began to withdraw into himself. He felt that he had failed as a father. He had lost his usual equilibrium, and nothing he did brought it back. He stopped calling prospects because he knew no one would want to see him. He even began to distance himself from his general agent and co-workers, and he put up a wall between himself and the family he so dearly loved. He had entered a

THE SALES SLUMP DOCTOR IS IN!

slump.

I needed more information and asked Tony if I could speak with this general agent. He agreed to this and I met with the general agent. I wanted to know if he was aware of what was going on and, if so, how he had attempted to help. He said, "I tried to reach him with motivation, but nothing budged him." Motivation? Motivation? That's a short-term fix for a long-term problem. (Motivation is discussed in greater detail in the following chapter.)

Fortunately, Tony's problem could be remedied. I will walk you through this one, but later in this chapter, and as I have done throughout the book, you will have the opportunity to solve the problems before seeing the solutions I used. His pain was so powerful that he was highly motivated to put up with all kinds of inconveniences to relieve the pain.

To begin, Tony felt he failed because his daughter got pregnant. He bore great guilt because of this and "knew no one wanted to see him." In truth, his guilt made him ashamed to see anyone. Crazy thinking? Yes, but nonetheless that is what was happening. I helped him work through this by letting him know how strong he was to stick to his beliefs about pro-life in the face of such a test of those beliefs. He had a strong religious faith, and I reminded him that God never gives us burdens we cannot handle.

Secondly, I met with Tony and his wife to help them work through their differences regarding what to do about the problem, and that was how they decided to raise the baby as their own, although they never planned to deny that it was their daughter's baby. This helped with getting him situational support. Also, I got him to go back to his church where he had become somewhat inactive, and I persuaded him to go to confession. This got him back to his roots and gave him even more situational support.

There were no actual coping skills that were needed in this situation. You might argue that Tony was unable to cope with his situation, but that is using coping skills in a broad sweep. When I use the term, I am referring to definable skills that are missing or skills that need shoring up to get him back to at least his former level of functioning.

Today, Tony, his wife, the children, and the new granddaughter are all living examples of a happy family. The mother of the child is a junior in college. The other children are all doing well in high school and junior high. The baby is four years old, and Tony and his wife told me that the baby made them young again. Oh, Tony is making more money than ever.

Always remember that when a salesperson is in a sales slump he is feeling a fairly high degree of pain, and because of that you can rely on him needing a fairly high degree of assistance. He walks into your office and says, "Please cure my pain." Because he feels the pain and wants you to cure him, he will be willing to put up with all kinds of inconvenience.8

Caplan stated that when a person is in crisis (slump) and equilibrium is not achieved ". . . some kind of adaptation is achieved, which may or may not be in the best interests of the person . . ."9 Resolution or non-resolution of the problem results in a new state of equilibrium, sometimes at a greater level of effectiveness and sometimes at a lesser level of effectiveness. Either way, new behavior develops.

"New behavior develops," what does that mean? It usually means that new coping skills will be developed, but it does not mean that these new skills will be to the salesperson's advantage. The goal of slump intervention is to return the salesperson to at least his former level of effectiveness in selling or to a greater level of effectiveness. Now just because this is the goal doesn't mean that's what happens. He could remain at a lower level of effectiveness. The difference here could be you. (Figure 6.1)

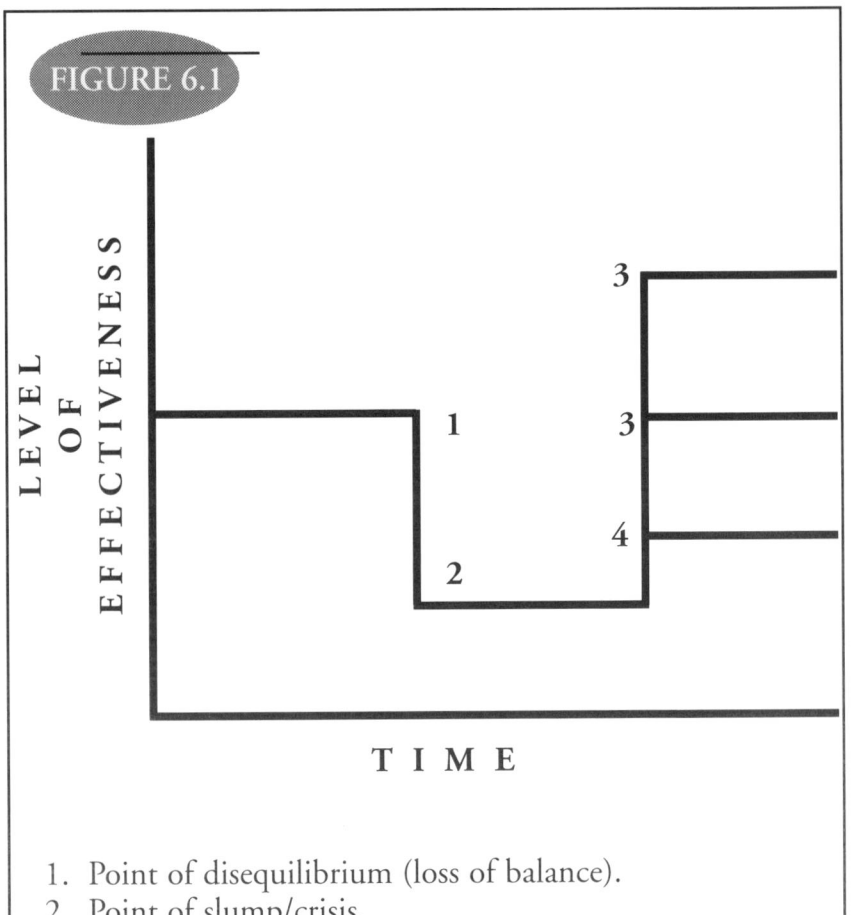

FIGURE 6.1

1. Point of disequilibrium (loss of balance).
2. Point of slump/crisis.
3. Point(s) of adaptive resolution.
4. Point of maladaptive resolution.

THE SALES SLUMP DOCTOR IS IN!

Let's look at another opportunity. This one does not involve anyone who has the title of salesperson, but as you know, everybody sells something. It involves a businessman and his partner. For the purpose of this book, we will call him Richard and his partner, John. They ran an upscale restaurant in a very fashionable part of town. Sonia, my wife, and I ate there several times a week, and noticed that the business was down, and that Richard was a nervous wreck. He couldn't concentrate, and his kitchen staff turned over almost as quickly as did his patio tables at lunchtime. He frequently would come and sit with us for a few minutes during our meal, and one day he was lamenting about his loss of business and the ever-changing kitchen staff when he asked if he could make an appointment to see me.

When he arrived at my office he was more nervous than usual. I asked questions about what was going on in the business. He stated that he was trying everything to improve his business. He had new chefs. He created and printed new menus that he thought were more in keeping with the seasons of the year. He redecorated the restaurant to make it more attractive. He even added a new room that could be used for overflow and special parties. While all of this should have made a difference, he stated that the business was still down. Oh, he assured me that he wasn't really hurting, but felt with the efforts he was putting forth the business should be better.

I moved on to what was going on in his life. The dam broke! Between the tears he told me that John, his partner and long-time companion, was using cocaine. He tried everything to stop him from doing this. He tried putting him in charge of the catering business. That didn't work. He created a to-go menu that they distributed to the businesses and offices in the area. That didn't work. All of this was to keep John too busy to think about doing cocaine. Nothing worked. He was at his wits end. He thought that every time the phone rang it was John's drug dealer if John was at home, or that it was the police if John was not at home. He even resorted to leaving the business to secretly follow John whenever he would leave. He did the same thing from the house. Richard knew his behavior was insane, but he could not help himself.

Richard was active in the community, and had a wide circle of friends. Those who knew what he was going through, and there were a few who *did* know, were there for him whenever he would reach out, but he did not often do this. When he was relating his story to me, he was convinced that he had managed to keep all of John's drug activity a secret. Living and working with a drug-addicted person is much like having an elephant in the house – no one might mention its presence, but everyone knows it's there! I asked Richard to tell me what, other than following John all over town, he had tried. He related what he had done to protect both of them financially such as taking John's name off all business and personal accounts, and how he had tried to keep John busy so he would not have any time to do drugs, but that none of this did any good. He admitted he was at his wits end. His fear was causing him great pain, and he was quite willing to do almost anything I suggested.

Stop! At this point you have all the information I had before I realized that Richard was in a slump – the sales in his restaurant were severely down and there were problems with keeping kitchen staff. Additionally, his partner and long-time companion was addicted to cocaine. Get your pencil and paper out to see if you know what needs to be done to get Richard back to at least his former level of functioning prior to the slump. Remember:

1. Perception of reality
2. Situational support
3. Coping skills

After you have written out your analysis of the problem and what you would do to change the situation, see if it agrees with my following analysis.

Richard's perception of reality was partially correct. He knew that John was using cocaine, and his concern for his business partner and long-time companion was to be expected. Anyone who cares for his fellow human beings would be concerned in this situation. But his solutions for getting the business back into a growth posture were not dealing with the problem. His problem was John. Not new chefs. Not new menus. Not redecorating. Not adding new rooms. Just John.

Situational support was there. Richard had many friends on whom he could rely – he just was not using them. He thought John's behavior was unknown to these friends.

Additionally, Richard did not know what help John needed nor how to go about getting it. He lacked the coping skills to handle this situation.

I mentioned earlier that Richard was experiencing great pain, and that I knew this pain would be very motivating. All I needed to do was to literally guide him into what he had to do to stop the pain. I did just that.

I told Richard that he and I and one or two of their very close friends who knew what was going on with John needed to meet to set up an intervention. His comment was what yours is at this moment – What's an intervention? You have seen this term throughout this book, and it was always used in reference to a sales slump. This time it is being used with regard to stopping John from continuing his use of cocaine. By definition an intervention is "an intervening or interfering in any affair, so as to affect its course or issue."

I explained that an intervention is where you gather a few individuals who were close to John and who were aware of the problem John was having with cocaine. They could not be his drinking or drugging buddies, and they had to be willing to get involved and to confront John with his behaviors.

After you assemble the intervention team you begin to gather data. This consists of compiling facts about the alcoholic's or drug user's habits relative to his use. You also need to have information about treatment facilities in your immediate area as well as those facilities that are out of your immediate area.

Each team member then makes written notes of specific incidents describing the user's drinking or drug use that give credence to the intervention. Each member's notes should describe in detail a specific incident that was observed by the team member writing the note.

Next, the team members rehearse the intervention. They start off by appointing a chairperson. Then they go over each item in the notes and determine the order in which each team member will read their notes during the intervention. Please note the word "read." I mean just that. It has been my experience that doing an intervention can become very emotional, and reading your notes will keep you on track. Now is the time for a dress rehearsal. You choose one of your members to play the part of the alcoholic or drug user. This person will become the Devil's Advocate during the rehearsal, and will bring up all the reasons he does not need help and that you are crazy for thinking he does. You then determine the proper responses to the objections brought up by the Devil's Advocate. This is good practice for the real intervention.

Now that you are all pros at presenting your story and overcoming the user's objections, you are ready to do the intervention. Where will you conduct the intervention? Any neutral location is OK, but I prefer to take the high ground – you know, a place where you have the advantages such as in your own office.

We went through the step to get ready and I-Day (intervention day) finally arrived. Richard brought John to my office where, in addition to me, sat three other people who were significant in John's life. Each related their story of what they had experienced while John was using cocaine, and how they felt when it happened. Before we were halfway through, John began crying and asked what we wanted him to do. He entered an intensive outpatient program where he went daily for two and a half months before being discharged into an aftercare program.

I am happy to report that today John is a poster boy for recovery and truly a partner in the business. They have also expanded into two other businesses.

For your review, I have included a chart graphically showing what was needed and what was done. (Figure 6.2)

FIGURE 6.2

ANATOMY OF A SLUMP

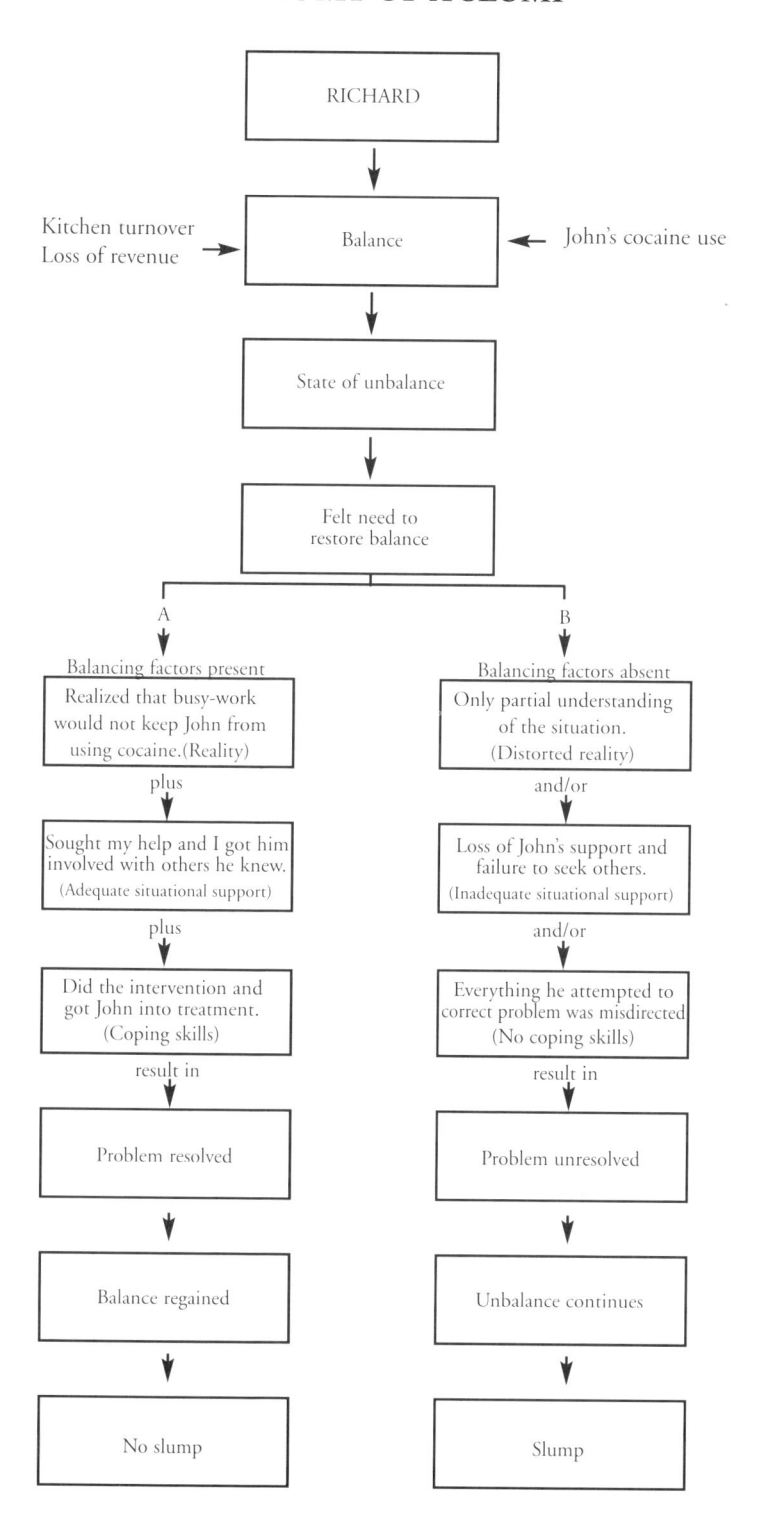

```
                            RICHARD
                               │
                               ▼
Kitchen turnover  →         Balance         ←  John's cocaine use
Loss of revenue
                               │
                               ▼
                       State of unbalance
                               │
                               ▼
                         Felt need to
                        restore balance
                          ┌────┴────┐
                          A         B
```

A — Balancing factors present

Realized that busy-work would not keep John from using cocaine. (Reality)

plus

Sought my help and I got him involved with others he knew. (Adequate situational support)

plus

Did the intervention and got John into treatment. (Coping skills)

result in

Problem resolved

↓

Balance regained

↓

No slump

B — Balancing factors absent

Only partial understanding of the situation. (Distorted reality)

and/or

Loss of John's support and failure to seek others. (Inadequate situational support)

and/or

Everything he attempted to correct problem was misdirected (No coping skills)

result in

Problem unresolved

↓

Unbalance continues

↓

Slump

CHAPTER 7

Motivation – A Short-Term Fix For A Long-Term Problem

Motivation – a short-term fix for a long-term problem. The lack of motivation is not the reason salespeople are not selling. They are not selling because they cannot sell. They cannot sell because they cannot organize their resources to utilize their innate motivational drive. To solve this problem you must get to the root cause, and that, my friends, is where slump intervention techniques come into play. How do you do this? It's as simple as ABC!

<u>A</u>wareness
<u>B</u>asic support
<u>C</u>oping skills

No, the rules aren't changing. I am just trying to make it simpler to remember. If you do not need this pedagogical device to help you, then use whatever provides you with the skills you need to help the person in the slump.

Remember, the minimum goal of slump intervention is resolution of the immediate slump and restoration of the salesperson to at least the level of functioning that existed prior to the slump period. A maximum goal is improvement in functioning above the pre-slump level.

Slumps are characteristically self-limiting and last from 4 to 8 weeks. This is a transitional period where both the danger of increased vulnerability to future sales slumps and where the opportunity for personal growth can occur. The outcome depends largely on the availability of help. Not just any help, but help in resolving the ABCs mentioned above. Remember, there are three possible resolutions to a sales slump: 1) the salesperson returns to at least his level of functioning prior to the sales slump; 2) the salesperson is unable to return to at least the prior level of functioning, and 3) the salesperson returns to a higher level of functioning than before the sales slump.

At this point you should be asking, "What causes these differences?" Before we discuss the causes for the different levels of recovery, we need to review what happens to the salesperson when entering a sales slump. Initially, pressures are brought to bear on the salesperson and this causes him to lose his normal state of balance. If this is the usual day-to-day problem encountered by most of us, it will be resolved and he will go about his daily life as though nothing ever happened. But, if the salesperson is bombarded by situations he cannot resolve he will lose his balance and, in the absence of regaining this balance, he will enter into a sales slump.

To get out of this sales slump the salesperson must go through the ABCs – he must have an accurate **awareness** of the problem, **basic support** from those significant in his life, and **coping skills** to overcome the problem. When these steps are properly completed, the sales slump is averted.

Let us get back to examining each of the levels of recovery from the sales slump. First, returning to at least the prior level of functioning. This is the goal of slump intervention. To reach this, the salesperson must regain his balance, and this is accomplished by following the ABCs. Let us take this one step at a time.

A represents the awareness of the true problem. Does the salesperson have an accurate perception of the events that are causing the continued loss of balance? In Chapter 1 – "Another Week Without a Sale," I talked about the feelings I had when prospects did not wish to see me. I became very paranoid and believed that they did not like me. The truth of the matter was that I was calling on builders during a building recession. They were not interested in life insurance. They were struggling to survive. My twisted mind conjured up all sorts of ideas that led to, "they don't like me." In truth, I was prospecting in the wrong market. To correct this, I had to be made aware of the problems builders were experiencing, and then to move into another market.

B represents basic support from those significant in our life such as spouses, salesmanagers, peers, friends, support groups, etc. These are immediate resources available to the salesperson in a sales slump. It has been my experience that salespeople do not make adequate use of these resources because 1) they do not see them as useful, 2) they do not want to bother them, or 3) they have alienated them by their pre-slump behavior. However, these people, who are most accessible to the salesperson, can be very helpful. They are readily available and already have some degree of relationship with the salesperson. Significant others can offer the much-needed emotional support to help the salesperson through the sales slump, as well as aid in the task of clarification of the problem. This stage of mobilization focuses on making the salesperson aware of these resources and helping him to make the best use of them.

Coping skills to do the job – these are the tools in the salesperson's arsenal to meet and overcome presenting problems. These coping skills can be as simple as turning a "NO" into a question or the ability to go through a complete financial program to establish a need. They are what separate the successful salesperson from the order taker.

Second, what happens when the salesperson does not return to at least the prior level of functioning? He did not regain his balance because he was unable to complete the ABCs. Something was left unresolved, and when the slump ended he was no longer functioning at his prior level of effectiveness. He ended up a taco short of a full dinner. This unresolved slump forced him to adjust to a level below his prior level of effectiveness. Maybe this new, lower level of functioning is more in keeping with his ability at this time, and will allow him to progress in a more realistic manner. So, is this bad? You must judge each recovery on its own merits. However, if resolution to the slump is not obtained, whenever the same or similar situation occurs, the salesperson will again go into a slump. It becomes a conditioned response – you know, like Pavlov and his dog.

Finally, what allows the salesperson to return to a higher level of functioning? In resolving the present slump the salesperson gains insight into a problem in selling and is then able to make a quantum leap forward. In Chapter 1, I related a story about an insurance agent who traditionally developed a sales slump every July and August "because it was too hot." I helped him realize that he deserved more money, not less, for those months and he went on to increase his commissions by over $3,000 per month. I am happy to report that this increase did not just occur during July and August, but it continued afterwards. I have since lost touch with him, but when I last spoke with him he had truly grown beyond this prior learned limitation that he imposed on himself. I suspect his income has continued to increase over the years. He escaped this self-imposed prison and went on to greater heights.

Motivation is defined in *The World Book Encyclopedia Dictionary* as "the act or process of furnishing with an incentive or inducement to action." Food is motivation to the starving person, but what happens when the starving person is fed? Warmth is motivation to the freezing person, but what happens when the freezing person becomes warm? We could go on and on, but I believe it is easy to see that what is motivating one moment in time loses its power when the person is no longer in need of the object. They then return to their prior state. Motivation is placing air under a balloon to keep it afloat. That takes constant energy because it is an artificial state. Remove the energy and it sinks again because you have done nothing to change its natural state. Slump intervention is filling the balloon with helium so that floating is its natural state. This is correcting the root problem.

Remember, the slump is self-limiting, and lasts for only 4 to 8 weeks. It is during this short-term window of opportunity that you can get the salesperson to face the dreaded "C" word: CHANGE. The pain is so great that the salesperson is willing to do almost anything to overcome the slump, and will usually accept your suggestions without hesitation. Therefore, it is essential that both salespeople and especially salesmanagers are aware of the

THE SALES SLUMP DOCTOR IS IN!

slump when it begins, and that they get help then. If not, it becomes a disability to the salesperson and a lost opportunity to the salesmanager. I have already discussed what can happen when a sales slump is left untreated. Let us look at this lost opportunity that the salesmanager suffers.

The pain of the sales slump makes the salesperson open to help – any help. Change, the thing usually resisted by most of us, will be welcome if the salesmanager reaches out to the salesperson during this window of opportunity. Good salesmanagers know what their salespeople need to do in order to grow, and this information must be readily available when the sales slump occurs. Yes, I am implying that salesmanagers must anticipate sales slumps and be ready to seize the opportunity. Too many missed opportunities like this are probably the cause for the great turnover in sales staff.

During a sales slump there is the danger that the salesperson can totally fail. There is the opportunity that the salesperson can soar to greater heights. Which is it going to be in your shop?

Note: For your convenience and use, I have attached a copy of the ABC worksheet that I also use when dealing with salespeople in sales slumps. I suggest that you copy this onto a sheet, make copies of it, and use it when you are helping yourself or others suffering from sales slumps.

THE SALES SLUMP DOCTOR IS IN!

SLUMP INTERVENTION WORKSHEET

Salesperson's Name _____

Date _____

AS EASY AS A,B,C

A = Awareness of the problem as the salesperson (or I if trying to treat myself) sees it.

Awareness of the actual problem, if different from the above.

B = Basic Support. Who do I/you look to for support?

C = Coping Skills. Change.

CHAPTER 8

You Can Live Through a Hostile Takeover and Merger and Come Out Whole

Everyday, TV, newspapers, magazines and trade journals bombard us with pending disasters, but many of these headlines are the outgrowth of progress. Any businessperson worth a grain of salt should be looking at all this as opportunities. Our doom spinners, the media, have everyone in fear of this progress – even fear of Y2K, which turned out to be less than a blip on the passage of time.

Machiavelli in his famous work, *The Prince,* must have been right when he stated, "It is better to be feared than loved ... Love is fickle but fear is constant." The media want us upset about these changes. That way we will continue to look for their guidance in these matters. It sells!

Headlines such as those mentioned in the title of this chapter cause stockholders to withdraw their support and stock prices to decline. Supervisors huddle together in fear and the workers are frozen out of the information loop. All this causes the organization to become unbalanced – second line management is no longer speaking with workers and the workers begin sensing their security slip away. When second line management go to their superiors, they are closed out and the cycle broadens.

Suddenly, rumors of mass downsizing begin and the downward spiral is underway. Workers have lost the support of supervisors – supervisors have lost the support of management and management is afraid to speak to the board for fear of causing trouble. Nobody is talking to anybody and the spiral deepens. It reminded me of a story sent to me by an early mentor that went something like this:

> There was an important job to be done, and *Everybody* was sure that *Somebody* would do it. *Anybody* could have done it, but *Nobody* did. *Somebody* got angry about that, because it was *Everybody's* job. *Everybody* thought *Anybody* could do it, but *Nobody* realized that *Everybody* would not do it. It ended up that *Everybody* blamed *Somebody* when *Nobody* did what *Anybody* could have done.

This is an all too familiar story today. I was a distant part of a hospital merger that began when the nuns who ran the hospital decided to switch to "professional management." Up to this point you never saw a smoother running facility. The medical staff got along – doctors talked with nurses, nurses talked with aids, maintenance supervisors talked with workers, and the nuns spoke with everyone.

Ten years ago when I first arrived at this hospital I recall seeing the CEO, a nun, bend down on her hands and knees in the lobby to clean up spilled water with her hanky. That was the prevailing spirit – if you saw something that needed to be done you did it!

Then came the MBA boys who entered the picture in the dark of night hiding behind their shields of secrecy. That's not just poetic, folks, that's the way it actually happened. They even moved the center of the operation off the hospital campus thinking that way no one would know they were there. However, everyone knew they were there, but no one was supposed to. That's how secrets are kept in big organizations. You know, like the king who rode through town in his absolute birthday suit. Everyone saw it, but no one said a thing. They pretended to see him in his new outfit. At the same time everyone continued to see what needed to be done, but no one did a thing. Everyone was too concerned with survival. They knew the MBA boys were only interested in the bottom line which interpreted into cut backs, more work and less pay.

I saw what was taking place and went to a highly placed vice president. I discussed the problem and the solution with this person, but they, too, were unable to function. The whole organization went into a slump and no one was willing to do anything to alleviate it. As a result, they never resolved the problems and they never returned to their former level of functioning. They dropped from excellent to just barely good. The trip down was quick because they were falling all the way.

The problem became so far-reaching that one day a janitor at the hospital came to my office seeking help to deal with the stress he was feeling over his insecurity about the unknown future. Then several nurses and a maintenance person did the same, as did the spouse of the new CEO's secretary. Insecurity permeated every level at the hospital and into the very homes of the employees.

Change is frightening even when everyone knows what is happening. But throw a cloud of secrecy over it and you are doomed – doomed to distorted thinking, doomed to lost situational support, doomed because you lack the necessary coping skills, doomed to go into a slump.

In earlier chapters, you read at great length about how an individual goes into a slump, and, if you do not already know it, let me be the first to assure you that organizations also go into slumps. The causes are the same, so are the symptoms, and so are the end results. The hospital I referred to was

THE SALES SLUMP DOCTOR IS IN!

unable to return to at least its prior level of functioning, and the air of suspicion generated by the early secrecy still persists. The following Anatomy of a Slump chart illustrates this. (Figure 8.1)

ADDENDUM

It is now the early part of March 2000. It has just been announced that the hospital merger is being dissolved! Will they learn from their past mistakes or will they plow on in their usual clod-like manner? Let's look at what they state is the cause of the split. They called it a "cultural difference." Of course this has nothing to do with the fact that one of the hospitals has a very high staff expense that is causing the other hospital to show a very, very small profit margin.

Of course I must finish this book before this new slump-causing event fully unfolds, but it is my guess that the hospital administration will carry on as usual, and that the hospital will once again go into another slump. It is also my guess that they will not recover to at least their prior level of functioning – which, of course is below the level that existed when the nuns ran the hospital.

Many of you work in smaller sales organizations, at least at the local level. How many times have you gone through a reorganization where everyone gets shuffled into new positions, or where territories are cut, or where you are moved out of your territory to make room for the new person, or any number of other changes. Have you noticed how production frequently drops throughout the organization whenever there is change? Oh, there might be an initial increase, but eventually it settles back to its former level. That's because nothing has really changed, or, as the French put it, *plus ça change, plus c'est la même chose* – the more something changes the more it remains the same. Workers are shifted around, territories are shuffled, more emphasis is placed here, and less emphasis is placed there. In other words, there has been increased activity in some areas and decreased activity in other areas, but, basically, nothing has changed. This we will call a Type 1 change – you increase or decrease existing behaviors/routines/systems.

Type 1 changes are resisted because they break our usual routine, but, in the final analysis, nothing has really changed. Type 2 changes are where we change to a different system, and that is frightening. Let me give you an example outside of the field of sales.

When you learned to drive a car with automatic transmission, you soon learn that you can exercise great control over the vehicle by increasing pressure on the accelerator and likewise by decreasing pressure on the accelerator. So you travel happily down the highway speeding up and slowing down thinking you have complete control over the car. Then a semi pulls out half a mile down the road and blocks the highway. You jerk your foot off the

THE SALES SLUMP DOCTOR IS IN!

FIGURE 8.1

ANATOMY OF A SLUMP

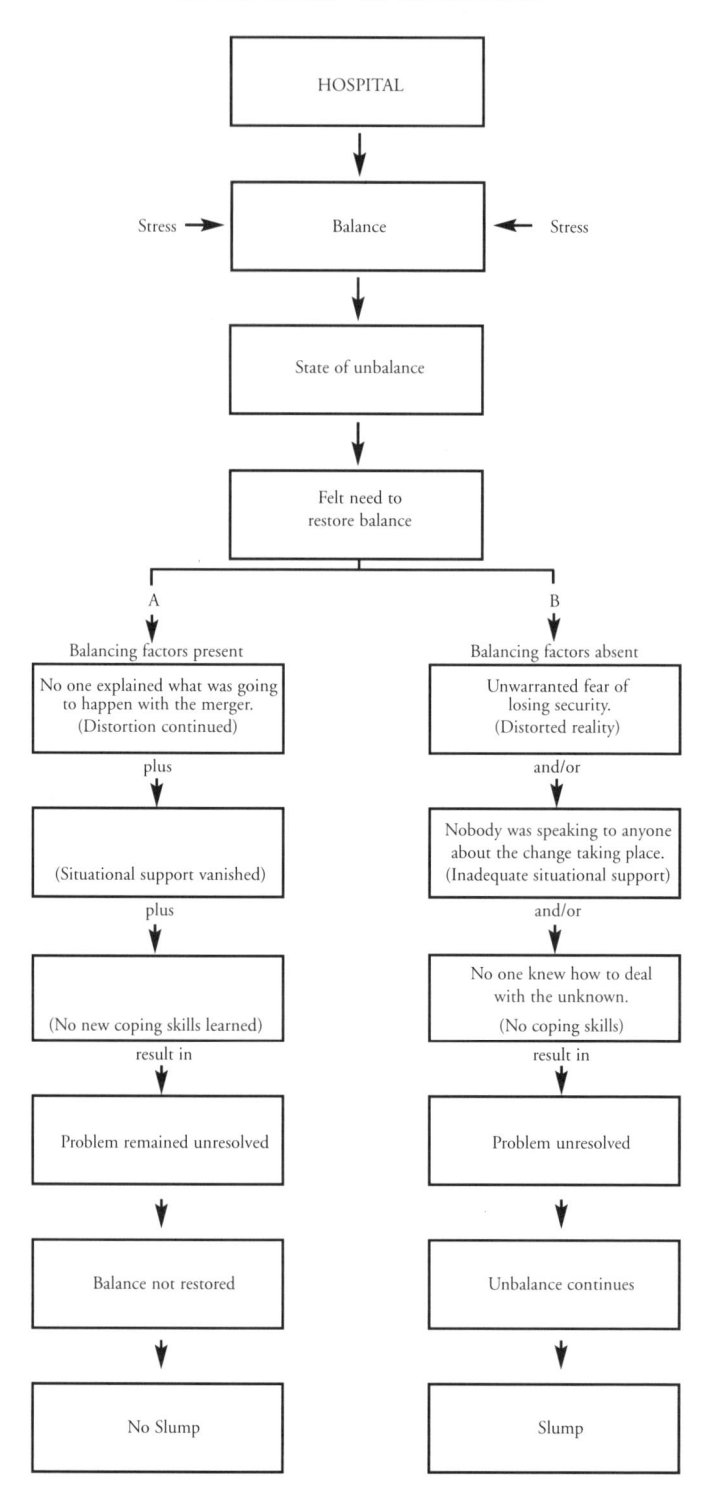

```
                    ┌─────────────────┐
                    │    HOSPITAL     │
                    └────────┬────────┘
                             ▼
   Stress  ───►       ┌──────────────┐      ◄───  Stress
                      │   Balance    │
                      └──────┬───────┘
                             ▼
                    ┌────────────────────┐
                    │ State of unbalance │
                    └──────────┬─────────┘
                               ▼
                    ┌────────────────────┐
                    │   Felt need to     │
                    │  restore balance   │
                    └──────────┬─────────┘
```

A — Balancing factors present

- No one explained what was going to happen with the merger. (Distortion continued)

  plus

- (Situational support vanished)

  plus

- (No new coping skills learned)

  result in

- Problem remained unresolved

- Balance not restored

- **No Slump**

B — Balancing factors absent

- Unwarranted fear of losing security. (Distorted reality)

  and/or

- Nobody was speaking to anyone about the change taking place. (Inadequate situational support)

  and/or

- No one knew how to deal with the unknown. (No coping skills)

  result in

- Problem unresolved

- Unbalance continues

- **Slump**

THE SALES SLUMP DOCTOR IS IN!

accelerator, but the car continues to travel forward at 55 then 50 then 45, etc., but you are getting dangerously close to crashing into the semi. You can increase pressure on the accelerator and decrease pressure on the accelerator, but neither of these Type 1 changes is going to stop your car in time. You need to leave this combustion system and switch to the hydraulic system, namely, the brakes. That is a Type 2 change. We will get back to this later, but let's look at another case.

WENDY'S CASE

Wendy, a single mother, sold computer programming for a large start-up company, and was very successful. She enjoyed a six-figure income and life could not be better.

One day rumors began about her company being taken over by a larger organization. No one in her company would admit to this, nor would they deny the rumors. In other words, Wendy was left in Limbo Land.

Pressure from not knowing began to escalate and she began to imagine all the problems this was going to cause to happen to her happy little family. Before long, in her mind, these imagined problems that she heard at the water cooler or at lunch with colleagues about job losses, etc., became her reality and she lost her equilibrium. When this happened she stopped making calls on her prospects and clients.

We know she had distorted her reality with these imagined problems. We also know that the company she felt "at home" with was keeping secrets. Under those conditions they were of no use in providing the usual situational support she had enjoyed from them earlier.

To make matters worse, this was the only job Wendy held since getting her children raised to school age. She was afraid of any change that would rock this secure boat she had built.

One of her old clients told her about me and suggested she contact me. She did, and I saw her immediately. I wanted to get in there during the opportune period when the pain was greatest. I listened to her story, and encouraged her to call the president of her company – after all, she knew him on a first name basis, and had been with him since the beginning of the company. She called, set up a meeting, and explained that I would be coming along with her. He agreed and we met.

Wendy explained her feelings, and I interpreted them to him in terms of Wendy's sales slump. He was very interested in what I had to say, as Wendy was his star salesperson. He also realized that if Wendy was having this problem, so might others in his company. Much to my surprise he engaged me on the spot to help him plan a meeting to explain to his employees that "yes, they are being bought," and "yes, everyone will continue at their present position." Actually, the company buying them wanted to continue operating this company exactly as it was without any changes except those that would continue its growth. Sales, which had fallen off, immediately began to soar. Everyone was back in balance!

They now had a correct perception of what was happening. Her boss proved his concern for her and all the other employees, which provided the situational support needed, and Wendy is now the head of a large sales team within the company.

If Wendy had not been feeling the pain generated by the uncertainty of the situation, she never would have called the president and her slump would have gone unresolved. She did not end up at a lower level of functioning, but she could have. Pain is grand – if you know what to do with it!

When a salesperson is in a sales slump he is feeling a fairly high degree of pain, and because of that you can rely on a fairly high degree of motivation. He walks into your office and says, "Please cure my pain," which was exactly what Wendy and all the other case studies presented in this book did. Because they felt the pain and wanted me to cure them, they were willing to put up with all kinds of inconvenience.[10]

Caplan stated that when a person is in crisis [slump] and equilibrium is not achieved ". . . some kind of adaptation is achieved, which may or may not be in the best interest of the person . . ."[11] Resolution or non-resolution of the problem results in a new state of equilibrium, sometimes at a greater level of effectiveness and sometimes at a lesser level of effectiveness. Either way, new behavior develops.

"New behavior develops," what does that mean? It usually means that new coping skills will be developed, but it does not mean that these new skills will be to the salesperson's advantage. The goal of slump intervention is to return the salesperson to at least his former level of effectiveness in selling or to a greater level of effectiveness. Now just because this is the goal, doesn't mean that's what happens. The salesperson could remain at a lower level of effectiveness. The difference here could be you.

DR. C FELT THE CRUNCH, TOO

One day at the gym, a physician approached me and asked if I could help him with his anxiety problem. I said "Sure," and asked him to call my office so we could arrange a convenient time for both of us to meet. He came to the office expecting hypnosis followed by lessons in self-hypnosis. What he got was something different.

He had an individual practice in a restored old house in the historical area of town, and was very successful. Managed care and HMOs continual-

THE SALES SLUMP DOCTOR IS IN!

ly carved away at his profit margin while increasing theirs, but he still made a handsome living. The hospitals where he performed surgery were merging, and they were pushing many of their attending physicians to form group practices in order to make better deals with the managed care companies. His was a unique practice in that there were only seven specialists such as he between the two hospitals, and they did choose to merge. Initially, it was interesting to have new colleagues, but he soon learned that he did the lion's share of the surgery, and, when you divided the dispersible income by seven, he ended up taking home less money than he did in his private practice.

Most people would conclude that this was a bad deal for him, and go back to their private practice, but he believed he could not survive in today's climate of managed care and HMOs in solo practice. Resentment of the associates who were getting a "free ride," and fear of the changing arena in which he practiced resulted in his feelings of anxiety – thus the desire to learn relaxation techniques.

A LOOK AT HOW I LEARNED THE EXACT NATURE OF HIS PROBLEM

When he arrived he began describing his symptoms of anxiety, just as I would expect a good physician to do, I listened. But not just to the words, but also to the emotions that were being expressed while he gave me the scenario of the practice merger, and the problems resulting there from. My conclusion from his presenting problems was to ask him "Why don't you leave the practice?" He was shocked at my question. "How can a solo practitioner survive today in the face of managed care and HMOs," he asked? "BINGO," I said to myself. His anxiety was resulting from his inability to regain his balance that was lost when the merger he was involved in did not gel as he had expected.

I then began exploring what situational support he had at this time. It was good. His wife was there for him, and his father, a retired physician, was his "best friend." He assured me that all the important people in his life, but for a few members of the merger, were there for him. This area got a big check mark.

Next, I examined his coping skills – his ability to do something to change his present situation. I discovered he still owned the building where his solo practice was located, and that he still practiced there two days a week as part of the merged practice. I also discovered that he had the financial ability to begin again if he had to rebuild his practice from scratch. Finally, I learned that there was no "non-compete clause" in the merger agreement, and that he was still seeing all of his former patients as well as many new ones. So he still had a strong patient base. That gave him another big check mark.

You might have noticed that I was using slump intervention techniques with this physician. He wasn't a salesman, as we know salesmen to be. How could this apply to him? To believe that this successful physician did not sell would require a rather narrow view of selling. What are we doing when we ask the campus beauty queen for a date? What are we doing when we debate politics? What are we doing when we "help" our spouse decide on the economy car rather than the luxury model? All of this is selling. We sell constantly!

WHAT NEEDED TO BE DONE TO GIVE THIS MAN RELIEF?

Before I give you the rest of the story, take a minute and think of what you would have done if you were in my shoes. This is good practice for you.

Now look at the chart. (Figure 8.2)

Did your analysis of the situation come up with what needed to be done? If so, I congratulate you. If not, don't worry – practice and experience will turn you into a pro in no time.

It was very obvious to me that the good doctor distorted reality when he believed he had to be in a group practice in order to survive the Managed Care and HMO era. A quick look at the yellow pages or the many solo practitioners thriving in the community would have told him otherwise, but, at the time, his reality would not let him see this. Too, his solo practice was thriving before he went into the joint practice – only his fear of the unknown caused him to join the joint practice.

Based on the answers I received about his perception of reality, his situational support, and his coping skills, I opted to only ask one question, "Why are you still in this joint practice?" His answers could not satisfy him or me. He smiled and said, "You're suggesting that I leave the joint practice and go back to my solo practice, aren't you?" My smile was a dead give away. He then rose and walked out of the office without saying a word. A week later he asked me to lunch. It was then that he told me he agreed, and his lawyer was in the process of getting him out of the joint practice. Two months later he took my wife and me to dinner to celebrate his return to solo practice. It is now two years later, his practice is bigger than ever, and he and his family are as happy as hogs in slop – to use an old Georgia expression.

I don't know if you surmised this from the above, but I only saw the doctor for one one-hour visit – lunch and dinner excluded. Oh, there was never another word about the anxiety.

In the beginning of this chapter, I spoke generally about fear of the unknown – change. I also spoke of how organizations frequently mishandle

THE SALES SLUMP DOCTOR IS IN!

presenting change to employees. Companies need to embrace change, especially when it comes to dealing with new technologies such as e-commerce, and educate themselves at all levels in adapting these changes to the way they do business. These are the changes that will launch your organization into the 21st century.

THE SALES SLUMP DOCTOR IS IN!

FIGURE 8.2

ANATOMY OF A SLUMP

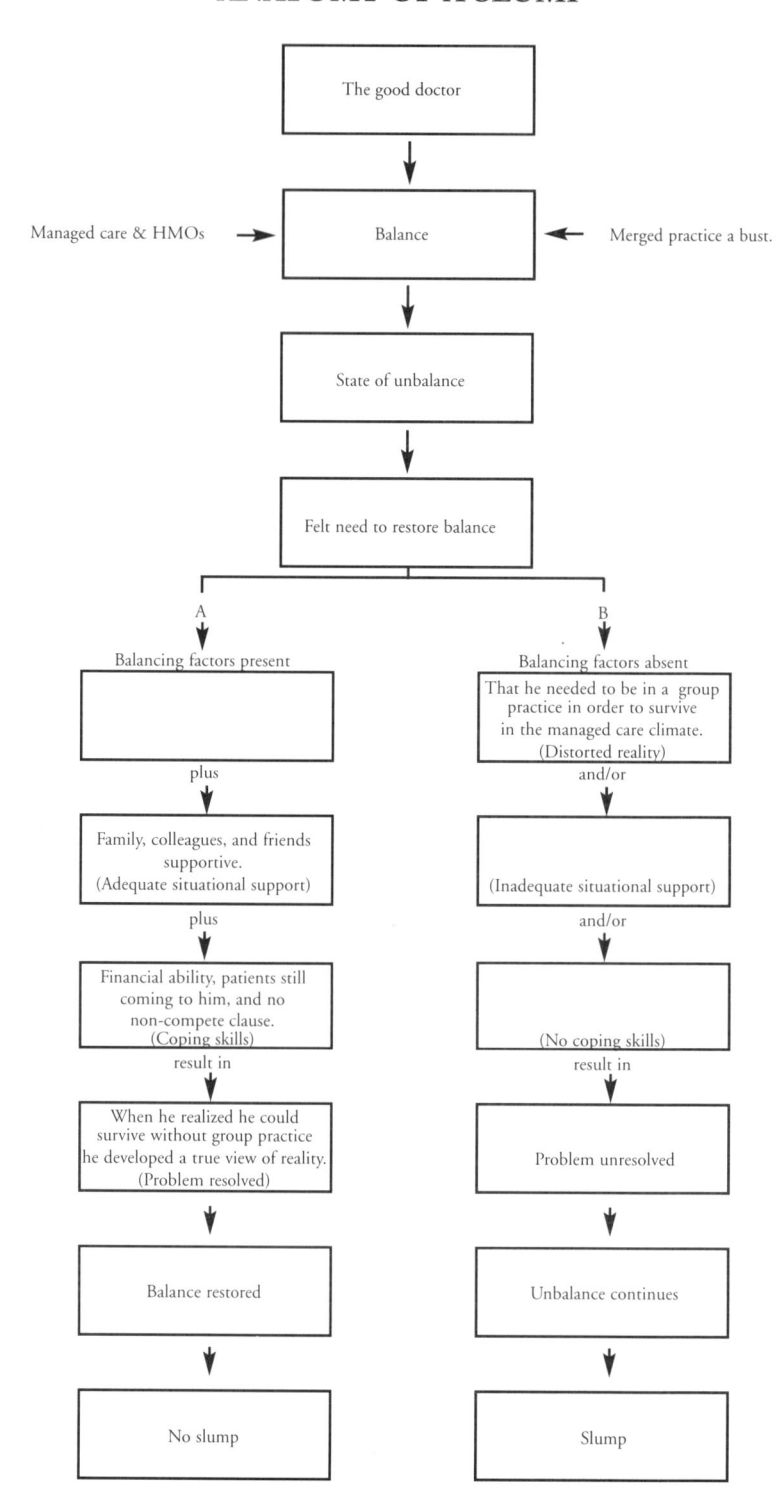

```
                           ┌─────────────────┐
                           │ The good doctor │
                           └────────┬────────┘
                                    ↓
Managed care & HMOs  →     ┌─────────────────┐     ←  Merged practice a bust.
                           │     Balance     │
                           └────────┬────────┘
                                    ↓
                           ┌─────────────────┐
                           │ State of unbalance │
                           └────────┬────────┘
                                    ↓
                           ┌──────────────────────┐
                           │ Felt need to restore │
                           │       balance        │
                           └──────────────────────┘
```

A — Balancing factors present

B — Balancing factors absent: That he needed to be in a group practice in order to survive in the managed care climate. (Distorted reality)

A: plus
Family, colleagues, and friends supportive. (Adequate situational support)

B: and/or
(Inadequate situational support)

A: plus
Financial ability, patients still coming to him, and no non-compete clause. (Coping skills)

B: and/or
(No coping skills)

A: result in
When he realized he could survive without group practice he developed a true view of reality. (Problem resolved)

B: result in
Problem unresolved

A: Balance restored

B: Unbalance continues

A: No slump

B: Slump

CHAPTER 9

The Rippling Effect That Sales Slumps Have on Our Economy
(a.k.a. Lost Opportunity Costs)

Do you know what a sales slump ultimately costs you? Get ready for an eye-opener!

The sales slump not only has personal significance, but also has specific and relevant economic ramifications, such as the effect it has on the creditors of the salesperson, and the creditors of the creditors, and so on. Additionally, it has social implications for the salesperson's everyday life, and in the lives of those who depend on the salesperson, such as: where do they live if they lose their house; where do their children go to school if they have to move from the neighborhood; where does the food come from? Questions such as these can go on forever, but bear in mind that we are not just referring to the immediate family of the salesperson, but to everyone who experiences the rippling effect of the sales slump.

Kilpatrick and Russ[12] state that, "Selling is essential for high employment . . . [and that] the typical salesperson . . . [is] responsible for the steady employment of 31 factory workers." When dependents are added, Kilpatrick and Russ state that one salesperson supports "109 consumers."

In 1890 there were only 264,380 salespeople in the United States[13]. In 1997 there were over 15.7 million employed salespeople with over 814,000 unemployed salespeople (Statistical Abstract of the United States, 1998). If what Kilpatrick and Russ stated above is correct, i.e., one salesperson supports 109 consumers, then over 88 million people are affected by these unemployed salespeople. That number, if true, is staggering – half that number is still staggering.

Other statistics are equally interesting. In a personal communication with LIMRA International (1999), they stated that only 15 percent of the life insurance agents entering the business survive the fourth year. What happens to this other 85 percent? Some seek greener pastures. Some decide that they do not like the insurance business. Most fail!

My own personal experience leads me to believe that the life insurance industry has the finest selection and training program in the sales industry. And despite this elaborate selection and training, their failure rate is exceedingly high. Why is this so?

I spent many years selling life insurance, and believe that I know the answer to this question. Most of the literature dealing with sales slumps approach the problem as one of motivation, positive thinking and action. Almost universally, sales managers try to motivate salespeople out of sales slumps with contests, trips, club recognition, etc., and they have been motivating good salespeople out of selling at a fantastic annual rate. You have already read the chapter on motivation, so I will not belabor the point by restating my position.

Let's take some time to look at what a sales slump actually cost. Naturally, it cost the initial loss of the revenue from the lost sales, but what about the long-term costs? A life insurance salesperson who was part of my Experimental Group when I did my research had an average base sales month of $5,276.96 and during the slump month his sales dropped to $792.48; a difference of $4,484.48. The loss to the agent was 55% of that amount or $2,466.46. Let's not even get into what this cost in loss of renewals or future referrals from these missed sales, but it does not stop there. What about the $4,484.48 per year in income to the company, and then the loss on the earnings of that money times the years the policy would have remained in force? This gets into huge losses over the normal life of a policy. Now multiply all this by the number of life insurance agents in slumps each year times the average loss during these slumps and the number becomes unbelievable.

But what happens if another agent gets into the picture? Did the salesperson lose the client forever? I don't know, and any guess would be pure speculation, but bear in mind that long-term losses can truly add up.

Now let's look at the bigger picture. Did this agent's family have to lower their standard of living during this period? Did the bag-boy at the supermarket get laid-off because of the loss of grocery sales to this family? As quoted above, one salesperson supports 109 others. These numbers get to be staggering. But we are not through yet.

Money spent circulates anywhere from 2.5 times all the way up to 7 times, according to which authority you cite[14]. I will be conservative and select 3 times. Now let's go back to the example above where the agent lost $2,466.46 in commissions, and let's assume, for the sake of this discussion, that he would have spent all of this amount on various items in his community. Using the factor of 3 times, the rippling effect of just this amount had a negative economic impact on his community of $7,399.38. Multiply the 3 times factor times the dollar loss of the number of other salespeople in sales slumps, and you come up with what I would consider the true financial cost of the sales slump.

But what about the other costs? We have all seen the effects a sales slump has on the salesperson. We have seen them mope around the office and

THE SALES SLUMP DOCTOR IS IN!

demoralize other salespeople who come in contact with them. And we have experienced the salesperson isolating himself, and staying away from everyone who could help. We have seen the weight loss that happens to some while others soothe their miseries with food – or worse yet, alcohol or other drugs. I have, unfortunately, been told of a few who have actually committed the ultimate act – suicide.

How does the sales slump affect the immediate family of the salesperson? In addition to the loss of revenue, the depression described above also has a rippling effect on the family. Everyone is exposed and it is catching. The spouse usually receives the brunt of it, and frequently feels that she or he is responsible. This causes them to become depressed, and then it spreads to the children. Before long you have an entire family suffering from this sales slump, which makes it more urgent that some resolution is sought. After getting this far in the book, you should have the tools to help. Will you be prepared?

CHAPTER 10

Stages of Slump Intervention, and What They Mean to the Sales Manager

Hey! What is the role of the salesmanager when one of his salespeople is in a sales slump? Don't know? Here is what he should be doing – going through the balancing factors to get the salesperson at least to his level of functioning prior to the sales slump. Better yet, help the salesperson to grow beyond his former level of functioning by learning new or better ways of doing things. How would you go about doing this? You would do this by working through the following specific stages during your slump intervention contact with the salesperson. Each stage is tied to the restoration of one or more of the balancing factors shown once more in Figure 10.1.

THE STAGES OF SLUMP INTERVENTION ARE:
1. Establish emotional contact with the salesperson
2. Clarify the salesperson's precipitating stress, current situation, and emotional states
3. Mobilize the salesperson's immediate resources
4. Develop short-term goals
5. Send the salesperson out to sell and/or refer, if appropriate.

These stages are explained below:

EMOTIONAL CONTACT

This is the slump intervention stage that zeros in on the formation of the relationship of the salesmanager and the salesperson during the period of the slump. This begins by the salesmanager verbally recognizing and accepting the emotional states of the salesperson. This could be something like, "I know you've really been trying, and it must really upset you when you can't close any of your prospects. Tell me about it." Such empathy establishes emotional contact and tells the salesperson "I care." The salesperson can now feel more at ease and begin to deal with the presenting complaint. The stage of emotional contact supplies the salesperson with needed emotional support and is one phase in the restoration of the feeling, emotional, or technically called the affective level. This really begins to supply situational support (balancing factor #2).

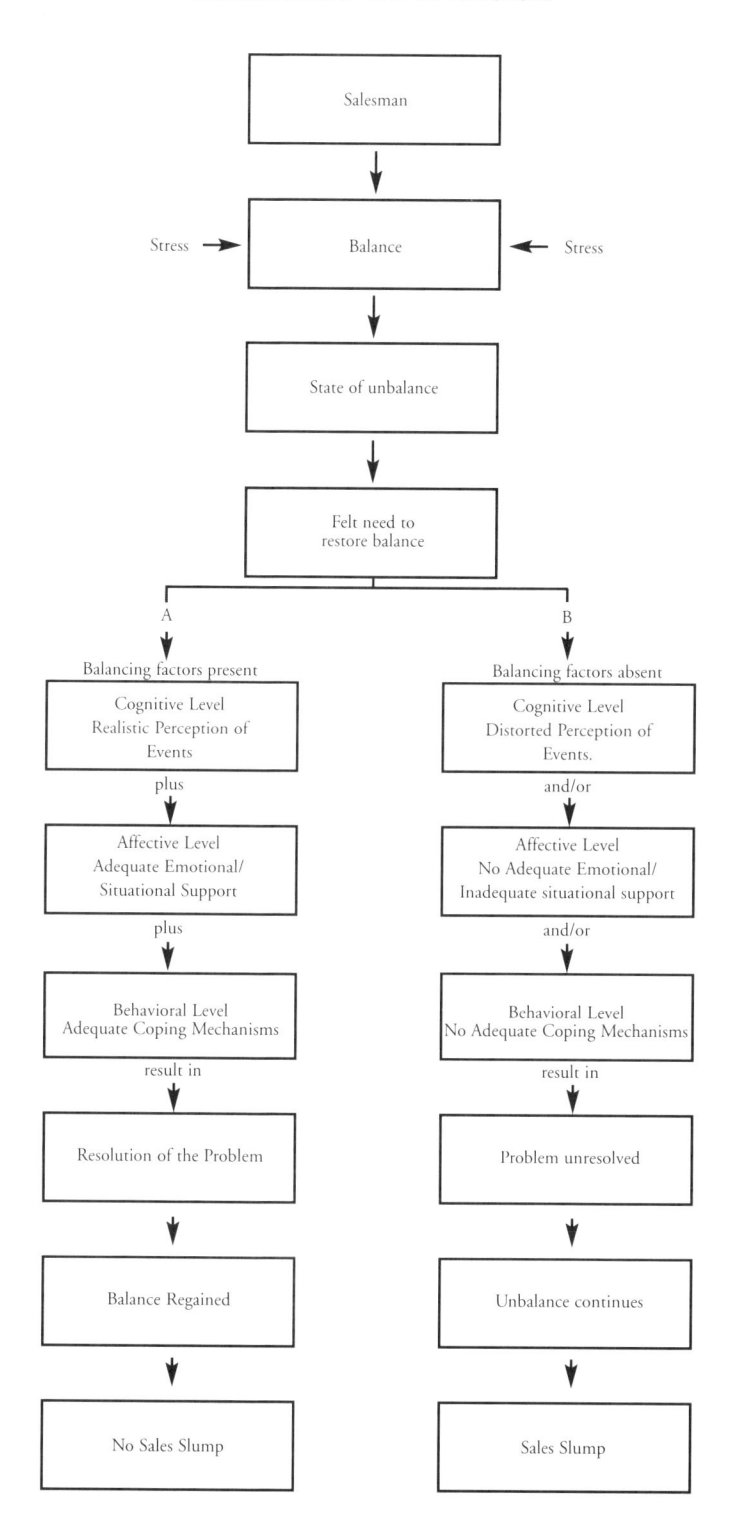

FIGURE 10.1
ANATOMY OF A SLUMP

```
                    ┌─────────────┐
                    │  Salesman   │
                    └──────┬──────┘
                           ↓
         Stress →   ┌─────────────┐   ← Stress
                    │   Balance   │
                    └──────┬──────┘
                           ↓
                    ┌─────────────┐
                    │State of     │
                    │unbalance    │
                    └──────┬──────┘
                           ↓
                    ┌─────────────┐
                    │Felt need to │
                    │restore balance│
                    └──────┬──────┘
                    ┌──────┴──────┐
                    A             B
```

A — Balancing factors present

- Cognitive Level: Realistic Perception of Events
  - plus
- Affective Level: Adequate Emotional/Situational Support
  - plus
- Behavioral Level: Adequate Coping Mechanisms
  - result in
- Resolution of the Problem
  ↓
- Balance Regained
  ↓
- No Sales Slump

B — Balancing factors absent

- Cognitive Level: Distorted Perception of Events.
  - and/or
- Affective Level: No Adequate Emotional/Inadequate situational support
  - and/or
- Behavioral Level: No Adequate Coping Mechanisms
  - result in
- Problem unresolved
  ↓
- Unbalance continues
  ↓
- Sales Slump

CLARIFICATION OF STRESSES, EMOTIONS, AND PRESENTING SITUATION

Clarification is the primary stage for the restoration of proper functioning to the cognitive (thinking) level. Effort is made at this stage to help the salesperson obtain a more realistic perception of his primary stresses, interpersonal relationships, emotional states, and current slump situation as it relates to these stresses, emotions, and relationships. The more realistic the salesperson views his sales slump situation, the better able the salesperson is to make appropriate slump reducing decisions and begin coping behaviors. Remember how in Chapter 1 I thought my prospects hated me when they would not give me appointments. When I finally was able to realize that I was prospecting in the wrong market, I was able to move forward by learning how to prospect in another market. This stage is broad in scope and attempts to obtain clarity for any area that seems to precipitate or prolong the slump. This includes any and all of the balancing factors.

MOBILIZE THE SALESPERSON'S IMMEDIATE RESOURCES

"Immediate resources" refers primarily to the salesperson's closest significant others (family, friends, salesmanagers, peers, etc.), but can include more distant relationships (physician, helping agencies, etc.). When in a sales slump salespeople often do not make adequate use of people around them because:

1. They do not see them as helpful;
2. They do not want to bother them;
3. They have alienated them by some pre-slump behaviors.

However, these people who are most accessible to the salesperson can be very helpful. They are immediately available and usually have some degree of relationship with the salesperson.

Significant others can offer the much-needed emotional support to help the salesperson through the sales slump as well as assist in the task of clarification. They are frequently immediately available and have some knowledge of the slump situation.

The improvement or re-establishment of communication between these significant people and the salesperson can greatly assist the salesperson's ability to cope. This stage of mobilization focuses on making the salesperson aware of these resources and helping him make the best use of them.

GOAL SETTING

This stage enables the salesperson to decide what needs to be done – what coping responses are needed. Goals should be set by the salesperson with minimal direction from the salesmanager unless it is needed. Goals need to

THE SALES SLUMP DOCTOR IS IN!

be immediately achievable, or very, very short-term and focused on resolution. Goals must also be action oriented so that the salesperson knows exactly what must be done for slump resolution. Do not get involved with anything long-term or that requires any great degree of planning. You want action, and it has been my experience that your salesperson will grab onto anything that will delay him from getting back into the game. This brings up the next stage.

SEND THE SALESPERSON OUT TO SELL AND/OR REFER

A salesperson in a sales slump is very open to suggestions and places himself in a dependent position when seeking assistance. It is important to remove the salesperson from this state of dependency so that he can again experience himself as an independent individual. When the sales slump is over, the salesperson is given a sense of closure and experiences that he is back on his own as an independent individual. If termination does not occur the salesperson is left feeling dependent and perhaps unsure of his ability to cope with the future.

Referral is made at termination if the salesperson is still in the sales slump, and your efforts have not been successful. The only problem here is to whom do you refer. To my knowledge, I am the only person who is currently doing slump intervention. This does not make it practical when it comes to referring. However, I do believe any crisis counselor who is willing to learn some of the basics of selling, and who is interested in this area, can do the job. Better yet, in the time you would take to teach a crisis counselor about selling, you could study the slump intervention techniques shown earlier in the book and become an expert. Then you could apply your newly found knowledge to the forms you will find in Appendix B and treat your own sales staff.

Each of the stages mentioned above is designed to assist in returning one or more of the balancing levels to proper functioning (shown in Figure 10.1.)

Figure 10.2, on the next page, shows the relationship of the stages to the balancing levels.

FIGURE 10.2

Stages*	Balancing Factors**
Emotional Contact	Affective Level
Clarification of Stress, Emotional and Situational	Cognitive Level Affective Level Behavioral Level
Mobilization of Immediate Resources	Affective Level Behavioral Level
Goal Setting	Behavioral Level
Termination and Referral	Affective Level Behavioral Level

*The Stages shown above assist in restoring the Balancing Factors shown in Figure 10.1.

**Affective Level = feeling level, which relates to *situational support*.

Cognitive Level = thinking level, which relates to *realistic perception*.

Behavioral Level = action level, which relates to *coping skills*.

CHAPTER 11

Forrest Wallace Cato Interviews the Sales Slump Doctor

The respected financial writer and editor, Forrest Wallace Cato, interviewed Dr. Greenfield, as one of the series of *Talks With Industry Leaders* appearing in *Financial Services Advisor* Journal. The Cato interview also appeared in *The Inspirator International,* the largest circulation English language magazine in the Pacific-Rim countries, as one of the series of *VIP Interviews.* This chapter contains highlights from those interviews.

Forrest Wallace Cato: Dr. Greenfield, how did you, a psychologist, become interested in the sales slump?

Dr. Mickey M. Greenfield: I was a life insurance agent for over 15 years, and for most of those years I was a Life and Qualifying member of the Million Dollar Round Table. While my career was successful, I rode the roller coaster most of the time – I either had a fabulous month or a disastrous one. There was no middle ground. Some 15 years and at least 50 slumps later, I decided to do graduate studies in psychology. In an introductory course, Dr. Bach said, "when a person faces a problem he cannot solve, he has a rise in inner tension with signs of anxiety and an inability to function in extended periods of emotional upset." He called this condition a crisis, but I immediately saw it as a slump. Needless to say, my ears perked up, and the good doctor had my complete and undivided attention. Did psychologists know something about the slump – the condition that has plagued salespeople since before Moses tried to sell the children of Israel the Ten Commandments?

After class, I cornered Dr. Bach to get more information. I ended up across the table from him at dinner, which extended into the wee hours of the morning. When we parted, we were both convinced that the term *slump* and the term *crisis* were synonymous. This sent me on a search of the literature, which, in addition to confirming my feeling that these conditions were identical, taught me how to treat the slump just as you can treat other crises. Eureka! I had discovered the wheel!

Cato: And after you "discovered the wheel," what did you do next?

Dr. G: I wanted to test my theory that crisis intervention would be effective in assisting salespeople in sales slumps. So when I entered my doctoral studies, I decided to write my dissertation on that subject. Before I could begin the research, I needed to obtain salespeople who were suffering sales slumps. To do this, I approached the program chairman of the local General Agents and Managers Association (GAMA) in Savannah, Georgia, and asked to speak at their next meeting. He was most gracious and made it possible for me to do just that. The rest is history.

Cato: What did you do with these salespeople?

Dr. G: I set up three groups of agents who were in sales slumps for the research. Control Group 1 was composed of agents who did not know they were being observed and remained anonymous to me. Control Group 2 was made up of agents who were seen by me and given psychological tests, and the Experimental Group was made up of agents who were seen by me and treated with crisis intervention techniques. They all had to be full-time agents with at least three years of experience selling insurance. If they did not weed themselves out of the business within three years, I knew they knew how to sell.

As mentioned earlier, Control Group 1 was not seen by me nor did they know they were being observed and they remained anonymous to me. Control Group 2 and the Experimental Group were seen by me daily for five visits. Both of these groups were given four psychological tests (one daily for the first four visits), and test scores were summarized at the fifth visit. Both groups were asked to bring me their production results at the end of 30 days. The Experimental Group, in addition to the testing, was given crisis intervention therapy on each visit.

The results of this research were astounding. In my book, *The Sales Slump Doctor Is In! The First-Ever Scientifically Tested Method For Ending the Sales Slump*, I discuss these results in dollars and cents in Chapter 1. In the book, you will learn what the sales slump costs you and your organization, the long-term effects of the slump, and how to end it in a positive manner. Most of all, you will learn how to remove this nemesis from your life and earn much more money, beginning immediately. Remember, this book is the first of its kind. No more whistle blowing or finger pointing – just scientifically proven methods for ending the sales slump!

Cato: What exactly was this "crisis intervention therapy?"

Dr. G: It's a technique that has been around for many years. What you do is make certain that the salesperson is viewing the problem realistically, has support from those who are important in his environment, and has the nec-

THE SALES SLUMP DOCTOR IS IN!

essary skills to take care of his problem. When you align these three areas, balance is restored and life goes on – usually at a level at least as good as before the slump and many times at a higher level.

Cato: How do you ascertain whether a salesperson is viewing a problem realistically? What kind of questions do you ask?

Dr. G: When they come to me, I usually ask, "What's going on?" The usual answer is something like, "I can't seem to get people to see me," or something relating to the problem as they see it. I then ask them to tell me about it. Both questions I ask are open-ended, which requires them to give me some information other than a yes or no. On one occasion, I thought the prospects hated me when they would not give me appointments. The truth was that I was prospecting in the wrong market at that time.

"Tell me about it" seems to be the magic that opens the door. From there, I can construct my questions to zero in on the truth. This comes from experience, much of which I obtained when learning how to find the money when selling. It's the same process – only the questions differ.

Cato: What happens if the salesperson does not regain balance?

Dr. G: Adaptation is made and the slump will end, but the salesperson usually does not regain the pre-slump level of functioning. This means that a new, lower level of sales results. Also, it has been my experience that whenever the same or similar circumstance that triggered the first slump recurs, the salesperson will again enter a slump. If the salesperson had help and regained his balance, he would have learned new coping skills that would stave off future slumps when the same or similar circumstances presented themselves.

Cato: Other than your dissertation, have you ever treated salespeople for the sales slump?

Dr. G: Yes. Several years ago I wrote my first article on the sales slump for Jacque O'Malley at Maccabees Mutual. This prompted several inquiries from salespeople, but I did not actually get into treating any until my articles were published nationally in *Insurance Marketing*. Then several salespeople called for help. They flew in for weekend crash sessions from all over the country, but primarily from the Eastern and Middle Eastern regions of the U.S. Initially, I would treat them individually, but I soon evolved into working with groups. This is when I was given the title of "The Sales Slump Doctor." I later became very involved in school and did not encourage further practice. Naturally, it tapered off, but companies heard of my work and have had me speak at their sales meetings. It's really a joy to have people come up to you after a speech and tell you how you have changed their lives. It's wonderful to be able to help those in need.

Cato: Is your method of using crisis intervention techniques to alleviate the sales slump something that can be taught to laypeople?

Dr. G: Yes. Across this broad nation of ours, thousands of lay people voluntarily man *Hot Lines* where people call with all sorts of crises. They range from a child calling for help with their math all the way up to potential suicides. I trained volunteers in Savannah, Georgia, to work the phones on the Help Line, a crisis intervention service. They were all lay people without prior training. We did it over two weekends. The first weekend was training, and the second weekend was answering the phones with an experienced Help Line volunteer on the extension listening and giving feedback at the end of the calls. I have offered similar workshops for sales managers, where they learned to use crisis intervention techniques to alleviate the sales slump. Part of the workshop is devoted to teaching technique, and part is devoted to practice.

Cato: How long would it take to teach a group of sales managers to effec-tively use this technique?

Dr. G: A two-day workshop is usually a good beginning. That gives about sixteen to twenty hours of intense work and practice. The workshop participants should then go back to their shops and practice for a month or two. Then, if needed, a refresher workshop of four to eight hours. I think it is very important that the sales managers have access to the trainer when they need help in a situation, especially in the early months of using these techniques. After every workshop or speech I have given on this subject, I have made myself available to sales managers or other trainers to help them hone their skills during the early stages.

Cato: Other than the actual crisis/sales slump intervention techniques, what else do you offer in your courses?

Dr. G: *Communication skills!* Before you can begin to help the salesperson in a slump, you must determine why the salesperson is in the slump. To do this, you must be a good communicator, and 90% of being a good com-municator is learning how to listen. I know this sounds basic, but it has been my experience that this is an overlooked area in management. You must learn how to phrase questions in such a way that the salesperson will open up and give you the information needed. Many times the sales manager will be speaking to the salesperson over the phone and not have the benefit of body language. How do you compensate for that? How do you keep the conversation going until you get what you need to help? How do you plant the necessary seeds of change? To many of us, this will be new. To others, it will be a refresher course. The entire second half of my book is devoted to helping you understand and develop good communication skills. Every workshop I present devotes at least 50% of its time to communication skills. Without them, we have nothing!

Cato: Where do you usually do the training?

Dr. G: Usually, a company or organization brings me to their location to train their people. That way I am able to learn about the company or organization and their problems as they see them. Then I am better able to address these problems while teaching Sales Slump Intervention. However, I have had small groups (five to ten) come to my office for an intensive weekend course.

Cato: Has the sales slump ever been scientifically studied before your research?

Dr. G: A thorough review of the literature revealed no existing scientific studies other than the study I did for my doctoral dissertation. In fact, there was no one definition for a *sales slump*. Everyone assumed the other person knew exactly what they were referring to when they used the term; however, my experience with salespeople proved differently. Some immediately thought of reduced sales, while others thought of the depressed feelings that accompany the slump. Still others had different ideas. When I first published articles on the subject, I was faced with the task of defining the term. As an operating definition, I said,

> *"A sales slump occurs when a salesperson functions in a capacity below his normal level of effectiveness relative to selling. There is a rise in inner tension; anxiety levels rise; and he cannot function over an extended period of time."*

This definition grew out of my fifteen years of experiencing sales slumps, my *Acre of Diamonds*.

Cato: In simple words, Dr. Greenfield, when does a sales slump exist?

Dr. G: A slump exists when a person is reacting to the stress of not making sales, and normal methods of correcting this have failed.

Cato: Are there stages in the sales slump that are recognizable?

Dr. G: Yes. Stage 1 is the critical stage—with all the stress—where the salesperson calls into action all the usual, normal coping methods. Stage 2 is characterized by lack of success in dealing with the problem using normal coping skills. Stage 3 is where the salesperson is forced to bring additional external and internal resources to bear. It is really an escalation of Stage 2. In Stage 4, we see major personality disorganization and/or behavioral problems.

Some of the factors that determine how serious the slump will be are character structure or the salesperson's self-concept, the quality and nature of past slumps (are they like or unlike the present slump), the amount of support given the salesperson, and his repertoire of responses to slumps.

The Manager's Task

Cato: What is the first action a sales manager should take when he notices a salesperson in a slump?

Dr. G: Talk with the salesperson. Offer assistance. Take them through the three steps mentioned earlier. I have a series of articles published in *Financial Services Advisor* starting with the May/June 1999 issue. I suggest you read or reread these.

Cato: If a salesperson is not receiving support from people in his environ-ment, what can a sales manager do to provide support?

Dr. G: The very act of talking with the salesperson can show your interest and concern. When you take the time to listen, you are saying, "I care." In my book, I have devoted many pages to communication skills. It is not only what you say, but how you say it that counts. As people engaged in sales, we should all be masters of the art of communicating. If not, shame on you. Getting back to providing support for the salesperson, remember: as a sales manager, you are already an important part of his environment.

Positive Results

Cato: Can a slump ever be beneficial?

Dr. G: Yes. The salesperson's confused state is fertile soil into which seeds of change can be sown, and they sprout and bear fruit in a short period. Resolving the sales slump focuses on strengths and brings them into action.

THE SALES SLUMP DOCTOR IS IN!

The salesperson learns to verbalize the problem and deal with it. This could allow him to detach and deal more objectively. New ways of problem solving are learned. By resolving a slump, the salesperson may reestablish himself at a lower or higher level on the effectiveness continuum – *one that may be more realistic* – thereby improving everyday functioning.

The Recovery Process

Cato: What percentage of salespeople experiencing slumps end up overcoming them and going on to greater success?

Dr. G: There are three possible outcomes for a sales slump: The salesperson is restored to at least his former level of functioning, is restored to a lower level of functioning. or is restored to a greater level of functioning.

What determines this is how the slump is handled. Remember, the slump is self-limiting and usually lasts from four to eight weeks. Due to this limited window of opportunity, you must act swiftly.

Most salespeople who resolve the three problems stated earlier return to at least their former level of functioning, and can go on to have successful careers. This is where most salespeople usually wind up.

When a salesperson does resolve a slump, he may not return to the former level of functioning. Sometimes this is not bad, especially if the salesperson is functioning beyond his ability. This adjustment can allow time for the salesperson to develop a more solid base of knowledge before moving forward. This, however, is usually not the case. In most instances I have seen, the salesperson will continue to go into slump after slump whenever the same or similar stimuli present themselves. This continues until the underlying problem is resolved. Then the salesperson is able to again move forward.

In the best of all worlds, the salesperson will grow beyond the former level of functioning by resolving the slump. While this is not rare, it is not common either. All this depends on how well the slump is resolved. As stated earlier, most salespeople resolve their slump and return to at least a former level of functioning. Some do not resolve the slump and continue to function at a lower level, and some soar to greater heights.

Cato: Mickey, in a few final words, what then is slump intervention?

Dr. G: It focuses on immediacy, and avoids long lines and the sixty-minute therapy session. It focuses on the positive or healthy parts of the salesperson. Its purpose is to get the salesperson back to the point of functioning in the company by utilizing his own support systems and those from the environment. The salesperson is contacted by the sales manager within the slump period and in the salesperson's own setting. Slump intervention develops new problem-solving methods and is not an overhaul of the basic personality.

Cato: Are you available for speeches and workshops on Sales Slump Intervention?

Dr. G: Absolutely! I have been making speeches and presenting workshops for much of my adult life. Some people tell me I'm a frustrated educator – others say I am just a ham at heart. I have trained thousands over the years in many subjects.

You can contact Dr. Greenfield through the *FSA* Speakers Bureau by calling toll-free 1-800-356-5936 or by writing me at 1820 Barrs Street—640, Jacksonville, FL 32204, or call (904)389-3784, or fax (904)389-4618, or send email to mgreen1932@aol.com.

APPENDIX A

THE SALES SLUMP DOCTOR IS IN!

Appendix A.1

ANATOMY OF A SLUMP

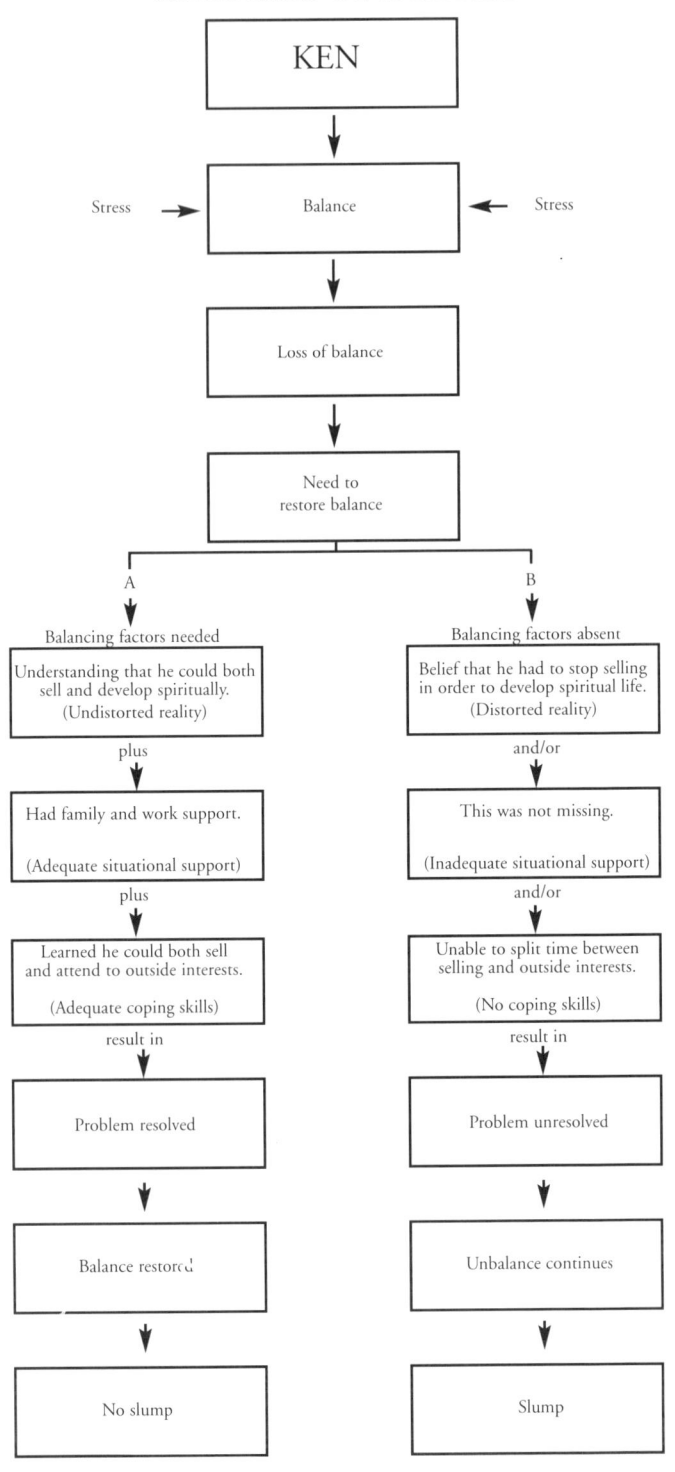

```
                            KEN
                             │
                             ▼
        Stress  →         Balance          ←  Stress
                             │
                             ▼
                       Loss of balance
                             │
                             ▼
                         Need to
                       restore balance
                        ┌────┴────┐
                        A         B
                        ▼         ▼
```

A	B
Balancing factors needed	Balancing factors absent
Understanding that he could both sell and develop spiritually. (Undistorted reality)	Belief that he had to stop selling in order to develop spiritual life. (Distorted reality)
plus	and/or
Had family and work support. (Adequate situational support)	This was not missing. (Inadequate situational support)
plus	and/or
Learned he could both sell and attend to outside interests. (Adequate coping skills)	Unable to split time between selling and outside interests. (No coping skills)
result in	result in
Problem resolved	Problem unresolved
▼	▼
Balance restored	Unbalance continues
▼	▼
No slump	Slump

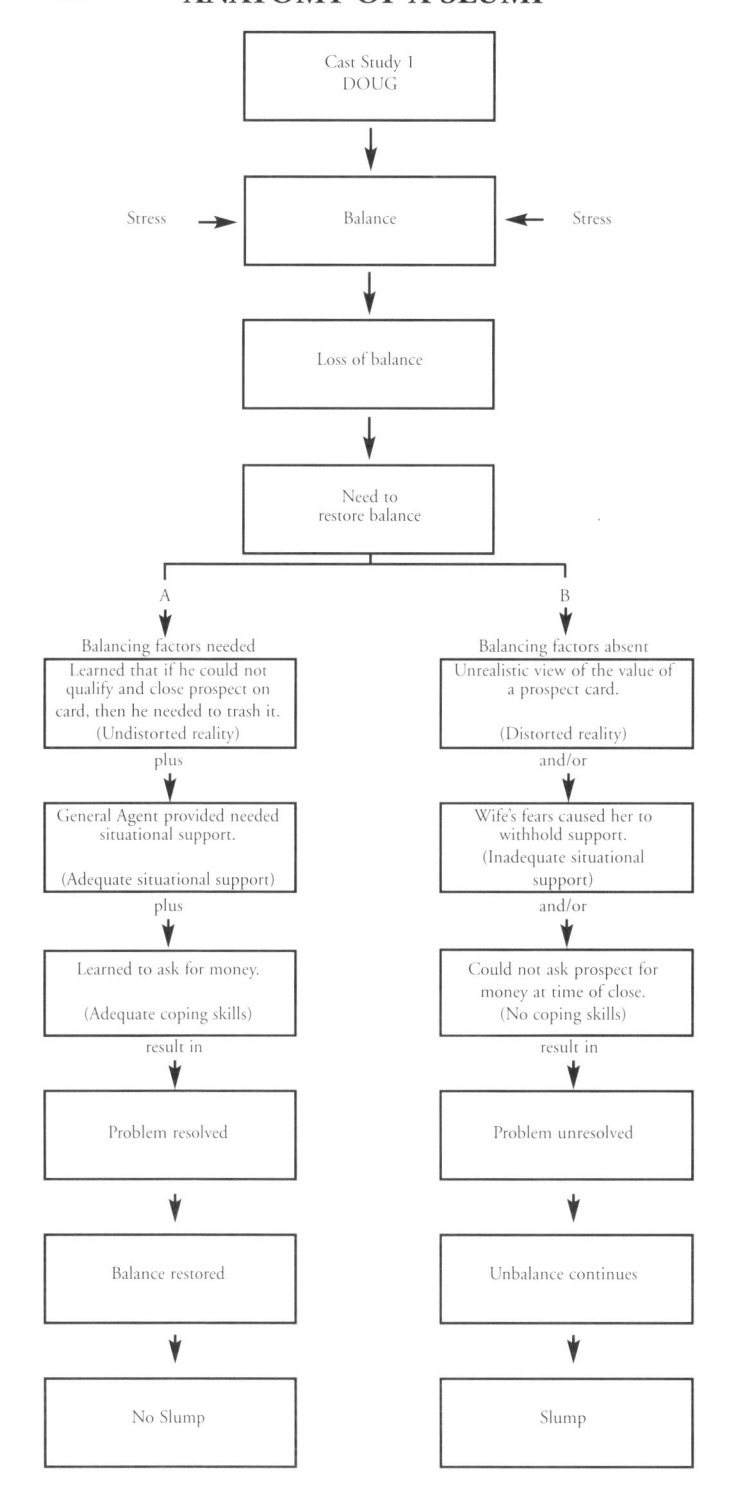

Appendix A.2
ANATOMY OF A SLUMP

```
                        ┌─────────────────┐
                        │   Cast Study 1  │
                        │      DOUG       │
                        └────────┬────────┘
                                 ▼
            Stress  →   ┌─────────────────┐   ←  Stress
                        │     Balance     │
                        └────────┬────────┘
                                 ▼
                        ┌─────────────────┐
                        │ Loss of balance │
                        └────────┬────────┘
                                 ▼
                        ┌─────────────────┐
                        │     Need to     │
                        │ restore balance │
                        └────────┬────────┘
                          ┌──────┴──────┐
                          A             B
                          ▼             ▼
```

A	B
Balancing factors needed	Balancing factors absent
Learned that if he could not qualify and close prospect on card, then he needed to trash it. (Undistorted reality)	Unrealistic view of the value of a prospect card. (Distorted reality)
plus	and/or
General Agent provided needed situational support. (Adequate situational support)	Wife's fears caused her to withhold support. (Inadequate situational support)
plus	and/or
Learned to ask for money. (Adequate coping skills)	Could not ask prospect for money at time of close. (No coping skills)
result in	result in
Problem resolved	Problem unresolved
▼	▼
Balance restored	Unbalance continues
▼	▼
No Slump	Slump

Appendix A.3

THE SALES SLUMP DOCTOR IS IN!

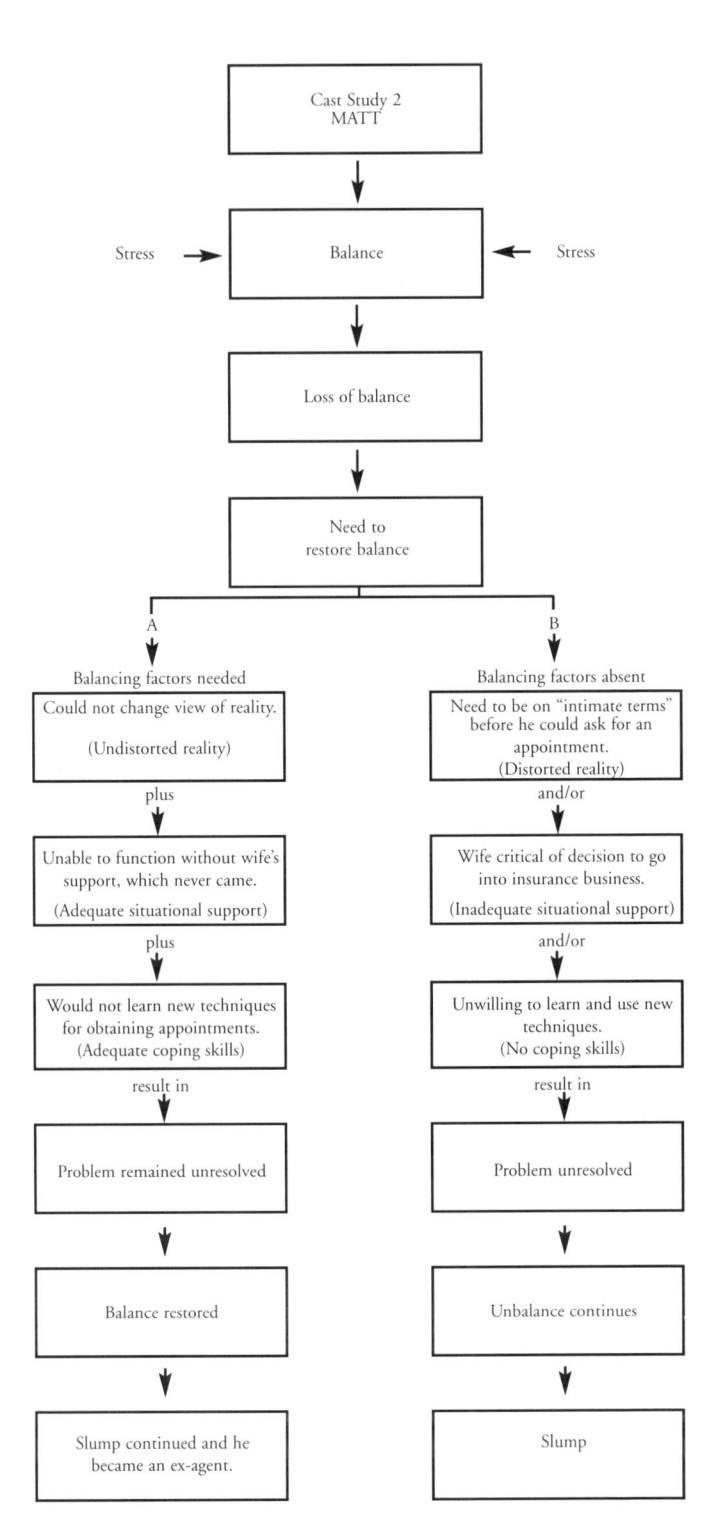

ANATOMY OF A SLUMP

```
                    ┌─────────────────┐
                    │  Cast Study 2   │
                    │      MATT       │
                    └────────┬────────┘
                             ▼
       Stress  →      ┌─────────────┐   ←  Stress
                      │   Balance   │
                      └──────┬──────┘
                             ▼
                      ┌──────────────┐
                      │Loss of balance│
                      └──────┬───────┘
                             ▼
                      ┌──────────────┐
                      │   Need to    │
                      │restore balance│
                      └──┬────────┬──┘
                         A        B
```

A	B
Balancing factors needed	Balancing factors absent
Could not change view of reality. (Undistorted reality)	Need to be on "intimate terms" before he could ask for an appointment. (Distorted reality)
plus	and/or
Unable to function without wife's support, which never came. (Adequate situational support)	Wife critical of decision to go into insurance business. (Inadequate situational support)
plus	and/or
Would not learn new techniques for obtaining appointments. (Adequate coping skills)	Unwilling to learn and use new techniques. (No coping skills)
result in	result in
Problem remained unresolved	Problem unresolved
↓	↓
Balance restored	Unbalance continues
↓	↓
Slump continued and he became an ex-agent.	Slump

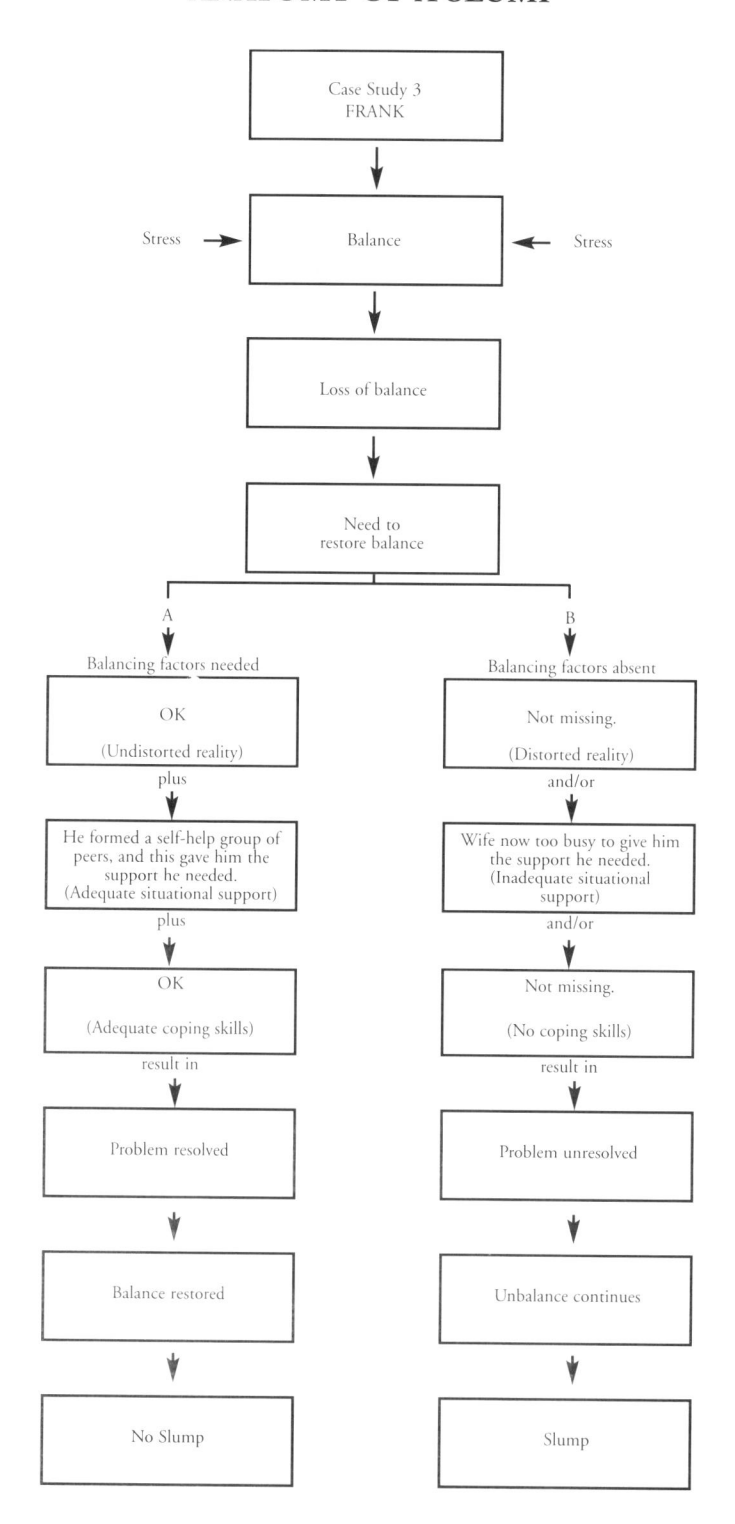

Appendix A.4

ANATOMY OF A SLUMP

```
                    Case Study 3
                       FRANK
                         ↓
    Stress →          Balance          ← Stress
                         ↓
                   Loss of balance
                         ↓
                     Need to
                   restore balance
                    ↙          ↘
                   A            B
      Balancing factors needed    Balancing factors absent

            OK                        Not missing.
      (Undistorted reality)         (Distorted reality)
            plus                         and/or

   He formed a self-help group of   Wife now too busy to give him
   peers, and this gave him the      the support he needed.
   support he needed.                (Inadequate situational
   (Adequate situational support)     support)
            plus                         and/or

            OK                        Not missing.
    (Adequate coping skills)          (No coping skills)
          result in                    result in

       Problem resolved             Problem unresolved
             ↓                             ↓
       Balance restored             Unbalance continues
             ↓                             ↓
          No Slump                       Slump
```

APPENDIX B

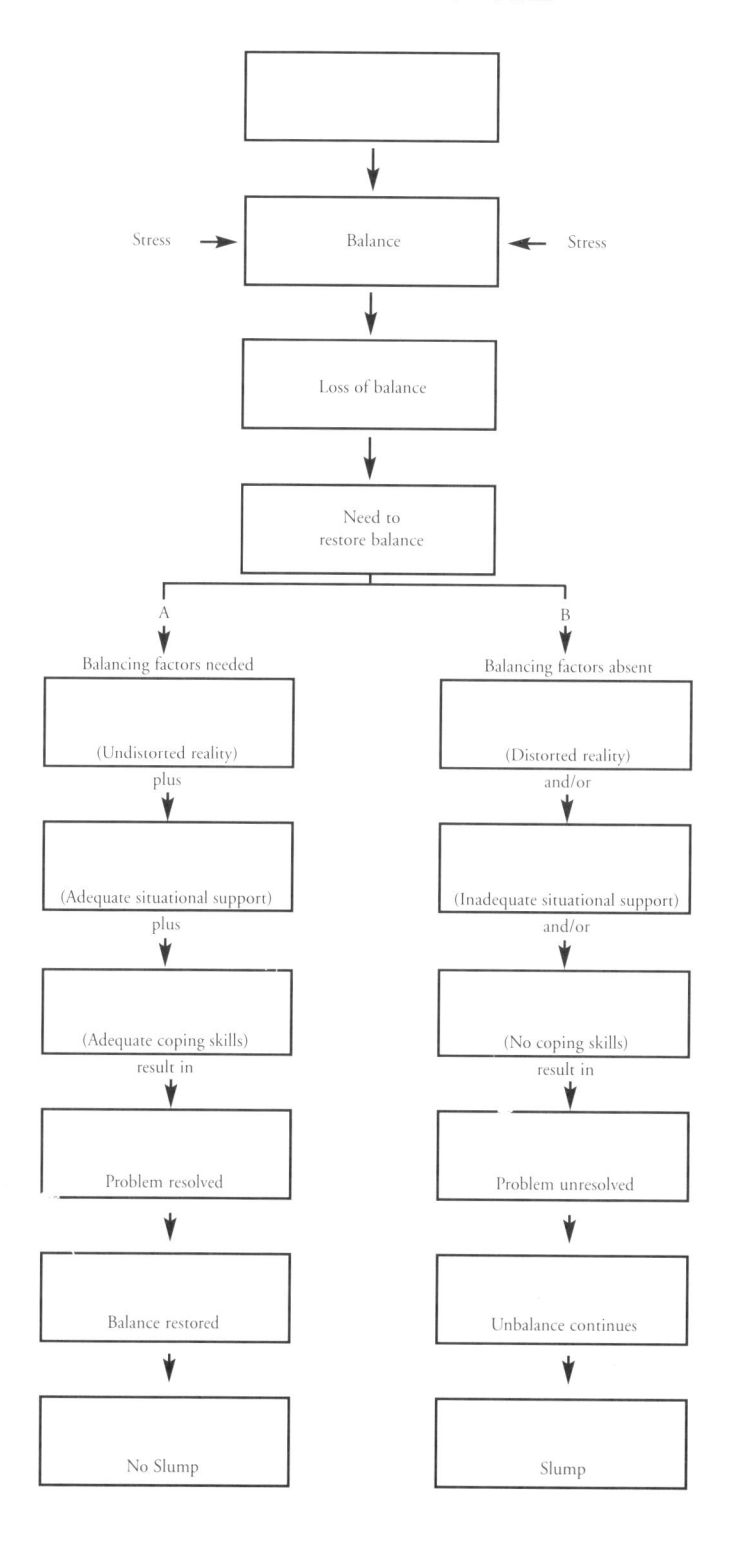

Appendix B.1
ANATOMY OF A SLUMP

```
                    ┌─────────────┐
                    │             │
                    └──────┬──────┘
                           ▼
         Stress →   ┌─────────────┐   ← Stress
                    │   Balance   │
                    └──────┬──────┘
                           ▼
                    ┌─────────────┐
                    │Loss of balance│
                    └──────┬──────┘
                           ▼
                    ┌─────────────┐
                    │   Need to   │
                    │restore balance│
                    └──────┬──────┘
                  ┌────────┴────────┐
                  A                 B
                  ▼                 ▼
        Balancing factors needed   Balancing factors absent
```

A	B
(Undistorted reality)	(Distorted reality)
plus	and/or
(Adequate situational support)	(Inadequate situational support)
plus	and/or
(Adequate coping skills)	(No coping skills)
result in	result in
Problem resolved	Problem unresolved
▼	▼
Balance restored	Unbalance continues
▼	▼
No Slump	Slump

THE SALES SLUMP DOCTOR IS IN!

Appendix B.2

SLUMP INTERVENTION WORKSHEET

Salesperson's Name _____

Date _____

AS EASY AS A,B,C

A = Awareness of the problem as the salesperson (or I, if trying to treat myself) sees it.

Awareness of the actual problem, if different from the above.

B = Basic Support. Who do I/you look to for support?

C = Coping Skills. Change.

Appendix B.3

SLUMP PREVENTION QUESTIONNAIRE

1. Where are my records, and are they current?
   _____
   _____
   _____

2. List three or more colleagues who have agreed to be part of my self-help group, and who have agreed to help me if I need them to do so.

   Name   Company Affiliation   Phone
   _____
   _____
   _____

3. Who helped during my last slump?
   _____
   _____
   _____

4. What did I do then that I am not doing now? Explain in detail.
   _____
   _____
   _____
   _____
   _____
   _____
   _____
   _____
   _____
   _____
   _____

1 Greenfield, M.M. (1984) The crisis in selling (Doctoral dissertation, The Union Institute, Cincinnati, Ohio, 1984). University Microfilms International, 8412901.

2 The experimental design was a Two-Factor Mixed Design: Repeated Measures on One Factor. The measurement used was an Analysis of Variance (ANOVA). The $<.05$ level of significance was adopted. Data reflected significant differences between subjects at the $<.005$ to the $<.01$ level, within subjects trials at the $<.001$ level, and within subjects times conditions at the $<.001$ level.

3 Kilpatrick, C.A. & Russ, F.A. Effective selling (7th ed.) (p. 65). Cincinnati: South-Western Publishing Co., 1981.

4 Greenfield, M.M. Sales crises. Insurance Marketing, 1979, 80(3), 30-31.

5 Caplan, G. An approach to community mental health. NY: Grune & Stratton, Inc., 1961.

6 As I explained in Chapter 1, the terms crisis and sales slump are identical for our purposes. Therefore, I shall begin using the terms sales slump or slump exclusively.

7 This is discussed in detail in the Chapter entitled The Lord Helps Those Who Help Themselves later in this book.

8 Caplan, G. An approach to community mental health. NY: Grune & Stratton, Inc., 1961, p.27.

9 Ibid, p.18.

10 Caplan, G. An approach to community mental health. NY: Grune & Stratton, Inc., 1961, p.27.

11 Ibid, p.18.

12 Kilpatrick, C.A. & Russ, F.A. Effective selling (7th ed.). Cincinnati: South-Western Publishing Co., 1981.

13 Wright, C.D. American Labor. In C. M. Depew (Ed.), one hundred years of commerce. NY: D.O. Haynes & Co., 1985.

14 U.S. Department of Commerce, Bureau of Economic Analysis and the University of North Florida, Department of Economics.

$12.95

If You Can't Say It, You Can't Sell It!

*Bonus Workbook

A Training Manual

Mickey M. Greenfield, J.D., Ph.D.
THE SALES SLUMP DOCTOR

Lexington House

Publishers of Leading American Books and References Since 1965

right © 2001, by Mickey M. Greenfield, J.D., Ph.D. All rights reserved. No portion of this book may be reproduced
m without written permission of the author. This is the exact text used in the Greenfield seminars and retails for $12.95.
Published by *Lexington House* ®.

Introduction

INTRODUCTION TO THE BONUS WORKBOOK

If You Can't Say It, You Can't Sell It!

It is my intent that this book will be used for the training of salesmanagers and salespeople to allow them to better help themselves and others overcome the nemesis known as the sales slump.

I suggest, that where possible, you develop a team to go through this entire book and practice on each other. In Book I you learned to easily identify the three stumbling blocks faced by all sales people experiencing sales slumps – a distorted perception of reality, inadequate situational support, and a lack of adequate coping skills. You also learned how to overcome them.

In the Bonus Workbook, you will acquire the skills that will allow you to ask the right questions to get the information you must have in order to help the salesperson overcome a sales slump. Without this knowledge you will not be able to help. (*Nota bene* – these skills that you will acquire will seriously improve your ability to sell!)

Everyone, but especially those engaged in sales, need to realize the value of being able to communicate. That does not just mean the ability to speak. It also means being able to listen. Someone once told me that being a good communicator is a four-to-one process – You listen four times more than you speak. I bet if you do this, not only will your sales soar, but just think of how popular you will be at your very next family meal. This manual was prepared to help you acquire this knowledge and to share it with others. It is an essential complement to this book, and is intended to take you step by step through the Trainer of Trainers Workshop on Communication Skills. This is what you will go through if you attend one of my Trainer of Trainer Workshops. In fact, it is almost the complete manual used. It does not attempt to provide step-by-step guidance. Room is left in the training format for individual style and ability to improve and expand the workshop. In fact, improvements on the workshop presented in this manual are encouraged, and I would like you to let me know what you have done and how it has worked. However, any modification should serve only to enhance the original intent of the training – not to change it into something it was never intended to be.

THE SALES SLUMP DOCTOR IS IN!

This workshop does not intend to prepare salesmanagers to be counselors and is not designed for people who are experiencing serious emotional crises. The latter should seek professional assistance.

Slump Intervention Techniques have been adequately covered in Book I, and the trainer can easily find examples in it to use while teaching the communication skills covered in this Bonus Workbook. After doing a few workshops, the trainer will have examples presented by the groups to enrich his own repertoire of examples.

Exercises have been set up to assist you in acquiring these skills and in the training of others. These are similar to the training exercises given to lay crisis center volunteers. They have been tried and proven successful in thousands of crisis centers around the world. I hope you will take advantage of this collective knowledge to better your life.

While I would like to take full credit for creating this Bonus Workbook, I would like to state that much of this material was gleamed from hundreds of workshops, lectures, books and personal conversations with possibly thousands of people like myself who have shared with me over the years. I cannot remember all the names so I will not mention any, but to all I send my thanks.

THE SALES SLUMP DOCTOR

Training Format

In this training manual, a strategy is defined as a method or skill. The workshop gives participants an experiential base in three strategies, which are essential to the successful use of Slump Intervention Techniques. Remember, if you cannot get the person in the sales slump to talk to you, you will be unable to help him. Milton Erickson, M.D., famed psychiatrist and my guru, said, "if you can get your patient to talk long enough he will tell you how to cure him." This holds true here. These strategies will also be helpful to trainers in carrying out all of their training responsibilities. The three strategies are:

Active Listening Skills
Listening for Feelings
Roadblocks to Communication

The presentation of each strategy follows a general format:

1. The strategy is introduced to participants with a brief overview, which explains what the strategy is, how it works, what purpose it serves (i.e., why we use it) and when it can be used most effectively. No strategy is presented as a cure all. It is useful in some situations, not appropriate in others. In short, the overview tries to give participants an appreciation of the strategy at a basic intellectual level.

2. Participants are given the opportunity to try out the strategy. Afterwards, there should be time for questions and discussion, with a special effort to point out other types of activities that could be tried, and to place the particular activity in the total context of that strategy. The workshop, as formatted here, allows participants only to sample a variety of activities. It is important to make them aware that they are only sampling – that there are more kinds of activities than the ones learned in the session.

3. Participants consider ways to use the strategy in training. Time may be short for this step. It is not essential to spend a lot of time here, since time is provided toward the end of the workshop for brainstorming. At least throw out one or two examples, so that your trainees can begin thinking in these terms.

Methodology

Training will be taught in two phases – the lecture/discussion phase where intellectual learning takes place, and the hands-on phase where actual how to do it takes place.

THE SALES SLUMP DOCTOR IS IN!

Using Energizers

As we all know too well, when workshop participants sit too long, especially after a big lunch, they become sleepy – the body is there but the brain is still out to lunch. Several energizers are included in the Appendix for such times. Be on the lookout in your studies and participation in other workshops for other energizers that will get people on their feet, moving, and awake. Whenever you use energizers, always do two things: 1) be sure the group is ready for the particular energizer you have chosen. If the participants are not yet comfortable with each other, use the Forced Choice energizer (no touching is involved). If everyone is relaxed, use "Back to Back" or "Knot." 2) Always point out to participants that they can use these energizers with their trainees, especially after lunch or in the afternoon.

Preparing for the Workshop

Nothing takes the place of good planning and preparation. Facilities must be comfortable and adequate to accommodate everyone and to allow space to split up for small group activities. Know something about your participants in advance. Know what you can expect from them. It is also important that your participants know what to expect from you. Well before the workshop begins, be sure the participants have a good idea of what the workshop covers. A workshop brochure is a good and simple introduction. Make certain that participants are clear on start times and ending times for each day/session. Plan a schedule to insure that adequate time is available for each activity. Keep in mind your objectives and how you will work to accomplish them. These and other considerations are often as important as the experiential training itself in conducting a successful workshop.

The Appendix also includes a section entitled, Tips for Trainers. These suggestions have been gleaned from a number of sources and are based on the experience of professional trainers. They are, however, just suggestions. You, as the trainer, can only be effective to the extent that you understand and believe in what you are doing. You are encouraged to use what fits your particular situation and frame of reference. Experience will be your ultimate guide.

Workshop Objectives

1. To avoid roadblocks to communications.
2. Learn to use verbal and non-verbal communication skills.
3. Develop skills in using verbal door openers.
4. Learn how to use clarifying responses to get the information you need to help the person in a sale slump.
5. Learn how to listen for feelings.

Session 1

SESSION I – INTRODUCTION/ORIENTATION

Introduction/Housekeeping
- Welcome – Introduction of Trainer(s)
- Brief Review of Schedule – "Comfort Issues"
- Review of Roles Participants Will Be Taking
- Purpose of This Session
- Rules of Workshop

Get Acquainted Exercise
- [Name Tag Exercise Can Be Used Here]

Pass The Symbol Exercise

A symbol or some tangible object is passed to the person wishing to speak. This tends to create order and facilitates the object of one person speaking at a time.

(Short discussion of questions that have easy, quick answers; address more involved questions throughout workshop.)

Community Building
- Double Circle Exercise
- Personal Goals For Workshop

Overview Of Workshop

The Introduction/Orientation session should not take over an hour.

SESSION I
INTRODUCTION – ORIENTATION

<u>NOTA BENE</u>: *This session paves the way for the rest of the workshop. It is important to build comfort as soon as possible, and to have this session reflect the experiential nature of the entire workshop.*

Introductions – Housekeeping

1. Welcome participants to the workshop – Introduce trainer(s)
2. Briefly go over the schedule – starting and ending times, lunch, breaks, etc. Explain the importance of beginning and ending on time to cover all that is planned. Explain that participants are expected to stay for the entire workshop. Go over location of restrooms, snack bars, telephones, where to receive messages, etc., if appropriate. It is a good idea to have the group establish a rule on smoking (e.g., smoke only at breaks). Also, NO CELL PHONES OR PAGERS!

3. Discuss the different roles trainees will be taking as they participate in the exercises. Sometimes you will ask them to go through an activity as if they were the trainees, then you will go over the exercise for them as trainers who will be leading it for their trainees. Also, they will be themselves and hopefully will enjoy some personal learning for their private lives.
4. Briefly go over the purpose of this introductory session:
   - To build comfort in the group with trainers;
   - To get acquainted with each other;
   - To get an overview of the workshop and the Slump Intervention Program;
   - To identify what they expect to take home from the workshop.
5. <u>Voting Exercise</u>: Purpose: To get general view of who the participants are.
   How many of you:
   Are familiar with the Slump Intervention Program?
   Have been through a Slump Intervention workshop in the past?
   Have been through communications workshops in the past?
   Have used role-play?
   Were told to come?
   (You may want to add others)
6. Allow a few minutes to discuss with those who were told to come how they feel about being here. Give them a choice of leaving, but explain that training is an important part of the total program. Express hope that the workshop will be better/more beneficial than they expected.
7. Have the rules for the workshop posted and read them to participants;
   - Only one person talks at a time;
   - When one person is talking, everyone else listens;
   - No put-downs.

You may want to substitute a set of "Corresponding Rights and Responsibilities" as your ground rules:
   - If you choose to answer, you have the responsibility to be honest.
   - If you choose not to answer, you have the right to pass.
   - Responsibility to respect opinions of others.
   - Right to have your opinion respected.
   - Responsibility and right to confidentiality.

Double Circle Exercise
(Purpose: to help participants become acquainted; to share feelings about the

program, workshop, training session, etc., to get participants moving and involved.)

1. Ask participants to number off – 1, 2, 1, 2, etc. All 1's form a circle facing out. All 2's form a circle around 1's so that each 2 is facing a 1. Ask the following questions, allow a few minutes for each person in the "pairs" to answer. Then blow a whistle and outside persons (the 2's) take one step to the right. Ask a new question.

   Suggested Questions:
   How did you hear about this workshop?
   How would you spend $100,000 (tax free)?
   How do you feel about using the slump intervention techniques?
   If you could pick a new first name, what would it be?
   How do you feel about being at this workshop?
   What is one thing you would like to change about yourself?
   What is something you like about yourself?

2. Process the circle exercise for participants as "trainers." Go over the purpose of the exercise. Ask how they would use this exercise in their sales organization. How would they modify the questions for their salespeople? Point out that it is a good idea to mix sales related (or task related) questions with personal questions.

3. This is the time to distribute handouts you will be using early in the workshop, if any, and explaining their uses to the group. At this point they can ask questions about the handouts and make their own notes relating to the handouts.

Name Tag Exercise

(Purpose: to help participants get acquainted, to raise questions relevant to being a salesperson.)

1. Pass out 5" x 8" blank cards or half sheets of colored construction paper, straight pins, and felt tip pens or crayons. Ask participants to write the name they want to be called during the workshop in the center of the card and embellish it as they wish. They should leave room to put other information about themselves on the card.

2. Give the following instructions (or make up your own items), leaving time after each instruction for participants to complete:
   - List five qualities of a good salesperson or sales manager around your name.
   - In top right corner, put name of a person who has had an impact on you.
   - In top left corner, put a skill (personal or professional) you would like to have or to improve.

THE SALES SLUMP DOCTOR IS IN!

- Across bottom, complete the sentence: "The most important thing I can do as a salesperson or salesmanager is _____."

3. Ask participants to mill around for a few minutes and to silently read each other's nametags.
4. Ask participants to form triads and share nametags (about 5 minutes). Discussion could be based on clarifying questions such as: "Who is the person who influenced your life and how are you different because of this person? How could you get or improve the skill you listed? Why are your five qualities of a good salesperson or salesmanager important to you – how did you come to choose these qualities? What were the reasons for your answer to 'the most important thing I can do as a salesperson or salesmanager?'" (You may want to post these questions on a flip chart or chalkboard.)
5. At the end of the discussion, ask each person to write on the back of his/her nametag: "One thing I learned about myself is _____" or "One thing I relearned about myself is _____." Ask volunteers to share "I learned" statements.
6. Process exercise. Go over purpose. Ask participants how they could use this activity in their sales organizations – what purpose could it serve? Brainstorm other items that could be included on the nametag.

Overview of Workshop

Have posted on flip chart the sequence of sessions that will occur in the workshop; go over briefly.

Pass the Symbol Exercise

(Purpose: to find out what participants already know about the Slump Intervention Program – to find out what they want to learn from this workshop.)

1. Pass the symbol to each person. As each person takes it, he says something he knows about the Slump Intervention Program. Each person should try to say something that has not been said. (You may want to record the information on newsprint.)
2. Pass the symbol a second time. As each person takes the symbol, he says one thing he would like to know when he leaves the workshop. Record on newsprint. Keep posted and address issues as they come up in the workshop.

Session 2

SESSION II – ACTIVE LISTENING/LISTENING FOR FEELING
Schedule (Total Time: 2 hours)

Introduction	(10 minutes)
Roadblocks to Communication	(20)
Active Listening	
Verbal Door Openers	(15)
Open Versus Closed Questions	(20)
Clarifying Responses	(25)
Listening for Feelings	(45)
(Presentation and Worksheet)	
Listening Skills with Subject Topics	(10)
Wrap Up	(5)

Handouts
    Roadblocks to Communication (4 pages)
    Emotional Vocabulary (optional) (2 sheets)
        Positive Feelings
        Negative Feelings
    Listening for Feeling Worksheet (4 pages)

SESSION II
Introduction

1. Ask participants to write their name several times on a piece of paper with the hand they do not normally use to write. Ask how they felt using the wrong hand. Explain that when we try something unfamiliar to us or try something in a new way – against established patterns – we sometimes feel awkward and incompetent. These feelings are natural.

2. Explain that in this session on Active Listening we will be learning some new ways of communicating that may be unfamiliar and may feel awkward. Point out that we learned the styles of communicating we use now by osmosis – observing people around us and unconsciously picking up their patterns. In the next section we will be consciously practicing a new style.

3. Explain that the most important part of effective communication is good listening. When we don't truly hear what the other person is saying, we are likely to respond in a way that may cause the speaker to feel misunderstood, pushed away, or putdown. When that happens you have lost the opportunity to help. In this session on Active

THE SALES SLUMP DOCTOR IS IN!

Listening, we will be learning ways to listen and to respond when someone else is trying to tell us something.

Roadblocks to Communication

1. Ask participants to think of a statement of opinion or feeling that they might realistically make to another adult. Give a few examples to get them on the right track:
   – I can't make ends meet anymore; I hardly have enough money to cover necessities.
   – I'm so tired of filing the paper work. I think I'll just get out of sales.
   – People today are so untrusting. I spend most of my time re-explaining my proposal and defending the numbers.
2. Ask five or six volunteers – one at a time – to give their statements. After each one, respond with a roadblock. Demonstrate different types of roadblocks. (See handout at the end of this section.)
   Example: "I can't make ends meet anymore."
   Response: "You'll just have to make out a budget." (Advising)
   "Everyone is having to learn to live on less these days." (Lecturing)
3. Ask participants if your responses were realistic. Might someone actually respond to their statements the same way? How did they feel? Were they willing to say more or were they sorry they brought it up? Point out that sometimes someone's response to us can make us feel misunderstood, inadequate – like we should change, or like our point of view doesn't count. Ask for a show of hands from those who have felt this way because of someone's response to them.
4. Handout the Roadblocks to Communication (at the end of this section). Briefly go over the examples of different kinds of roadblocks. Indicate the different kinds of roadblocks you used when responding to their statements. Explain that we all use them and we have them used on us frequently.

Active Listening (Verbal Door Openers)

(Purpose: these exercises introduce participants to the simple, first step in good listening – paying attention to what is being said, and showing the speaker that you are interested.)

1. Explain the purpose of these next exercises. Ask participants to think of someone they consider a good listener. What does he do that makes him a good listener? Ask for characteristics and write these on the chalkboard or flip chart.
2. Point out that we can show someone that we want to listen with very

little effort and no new skills. Often something as simple as body language can communicate our willingness to listen. Go over what you mean by body language: nodding of the head, good eye contact, interested facial expression, attentive posture.
3. Introduce the idea of verbal door openers – simple phrases that invite the speaker to say more:
"I see"
"Really"
"Oh"
"Tell me about it"
4. *Exercise:* (The purpose of this exercise is to have participants consciously experience listening and being listened to through simple body language and verbal door openers.)

Divide participants into pairs, one person is the listener and the other person is the speaker. The speaker talks for 2 to 3 minutes about a trainer selected topic, e.g., "My most embarrassing moment" or " The thing I like most about sales." The listener responds with positive body language and verbal door openers. Discuss the feelings that the listener and the speaker had during the exercise. Ask participants to think of some verbal door closers.

OPEN VERSUS CLOSED QUESTIONS

Trainees are given a brief lecture on open versus closed questions, which is followed by two trainers modeling the use of open and closed questions in an interview situation. Trainer A's task is to find out about Trainer B during a three to five minute interview; however, Trainer A is limited to the use of only closed questions to get information. After several minutes, when it becomes obvious that Trainer A has run out of closed questions and is becoming uncomfortable, role-play is stopped. Trainer A now repeats the same interview process but this time must use only open questions. The contrast in style and information is evident.

Trainees are now placed in pairs and put through the same exercise. They are given the task of getting to know their partners. One trainee begins the role-play as an interviewer but must ask only closed questions. After several minutes the interviewer is stopped and then repeats the same process using open questions. After several more minutes the role-play is ended and the partners switch roles. (Each becomes the interviewer and each becomes the interviewee.) The training procedure is repeated again with both closed and open questions.

A discussion is held following the exercise. Trainees are asked to compare

THE SALES SLUMP DOCTOR IS IN!

and contrast their feelings when asked only closed or only open questions. These feelings are listed on a chalkboard and usually reveal a negative, controlled, interrogated reaction to closed questions and a more positive, open, spontaneous reaction to open questions. Depending upon the predominant mode of questioning employed, these reactions are also experienced by salespeople when salesmanagers interview them.

The goals of this exercise are:
1. to help trainees distinguish between open and closed questions,
2. to demonstrate the difficulty of formulating open questions and the tendency to use closed questions, and
3. to illustrate the control and direction of closed questions.

Active Listening (Clarifying Responses)

(Purpose: these exercises introduce participants to a more advanced step in good listening – responding to the speaker in a way that he will know that he has been heard and what he said has not been judged.)

1. Explain to participants that in the next exercises, they will become more active in their listening. They will learn ways to communicate not only that they want to listen, but also that they want to understand what is being said.

2. Go over clarifying responses with participants. Explain that everything we hear or see we interpret by our own frame of reference before we can act or respond. Sometimes our interpretations are not accurate. When we are actively listening to someone, we need to check the accuracy of what we are hearing. Ways we can respond to get clarification include:

   <u>Paraphrasing</u> – restating the other person's expressed idea in your own words without judgment or interpretation of the content.
       Example phrase: "Are you saying . . .?" (restate in other words)

   <u>Summarizing</u> – expressing the essence of the other person's thought in a few words, especially before stating your own message.
       Example phrase: "I heard you say . . ." (then summarize)

   <u>Advance Tentative Examples</u> – stating a specific example of a general statement made by the other person.
       Example phrase: "Would this be an example?" (then state one) or "Does that include . . . ?"

   <u>Requesting Further Information</u> – If you are unable to do any of the above, then you need to hear more about the message, so ask for more information.

Example phrase: "I'm not sure I understand; would you say more."

3. Go through each type of clarifying response giving a concrete example of a statement and response. You may ask volunteers to make statements that you respond to. Examples:

   Statement: I could not do my report last night.

   Paraphrase: Are you saying that you did not understand the assignment?

   Statement: I understood what we were supposed to do, but I could not solve the problem.

   Tentative Example: Does that include the first part that we discussed yesterday?

   Statement: No, I see how to work that one, but I can't go on from there.

   Summarizing: So you're saying that you understand the first problem solving technique, but you don't understand how to use it to resolve other problems?

   Statement: That's right.

   Requesting Further Information: Can you tell me more about what you don't understand? Do you get to a certain point and then bog down?

4. Throw out three or four statements (one at a time) and ask volunteers to respond with clarifying responses. (Make your examples appropriate for the group.)

5. Divide the group into pairs (or keep the pairs you used earlier, but reverse speaker/listener roles). Assign the topic: "Feelings can surely affect what happens in the sales arena." Ask the listener to practice using clarifying responses. Discuss the following questions:
   – How did it make you feel to make a statement and have your partner clarify it?
   – Did it make you feel like he was really listening?

THE SALES SLUMP DOCTOR IS IN!

– How did it feel to clarify a statement made by your partner?
– Did you find yourself thinking about what was being said to you?
– How can you use these ways of responding in you office/sales?

Listening for Feelings

1. Explain to participants that Listening for Feeling is also a type of clarifying response; however, the emphasis of previous exercises has been on the content of messages. Listening for Feeling includes understanding what the speaker is saying, AND identifying, accepting and verbalizing the feelings that the speaker is experiencing. Listening for Feeling brings feelings out into the open. Without an active effort to bring feelings out into the open, they often remain hidden. The reasons for this include:
    - Many people are ashamed of their own feelings or believe that it is not proper to express emotions.
    - Many people believe that the listener will not accept their feelings.
    - Many people are not aware of their own feelings or are unable to define the source of their general discomfort.

2. Explain to participants that very often our true feelings are hidden just under the words we say. We tend to code our feelings, and the listener has to decode our message. On a flip chart or chalkboard, diagram this process.

    Example: One of your trainees is feeling a lot of anxiety about his work because he is reading ahead and realizes how much work it is going to take to catch up.

SENDER

ANXIETY | CODING | "Are we going to have give this to our manager today?"
 | | (CODE)

When you, the receiver, receive the message, you must go through a decoding process to enable you to understand what is going on inside the speaker. The decoding process must be a guess, because you, as the receiver, cannot see inside the speaker's mind.

SENDER   **RECEIVER**

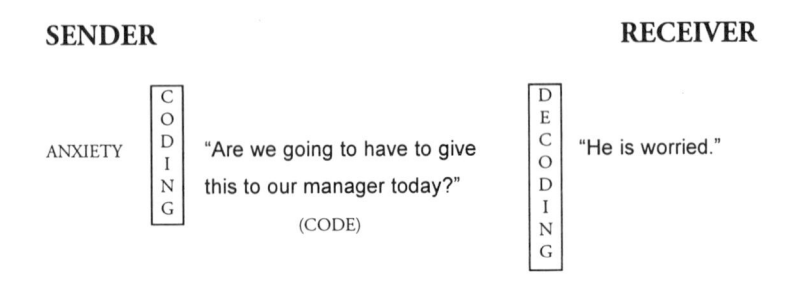

ANXIETY → [CODING] → "Are we going to have to give this to our manager today?" (CODE) → [DECODING] → "He is worried."

You cannot know if your decoding is accurate until you reflect the feeling you have sensed back to the speaker. More importantly, the speaker cannot know if you truly heard his hidden message without your response.

SENDER   **RECEIVER**

ANXIETY → [CODING] → "Are we going to have to give this to our manager today?" (CODE) → [DECODING] → "He is worried."

FEEDBACK

"You are worried about making your sales presentation to your sales manager today."

3. Go over the steps in Listening for Feeling: (Have these posted on the chalkboard or flip chart.)

– *The first step* is to try to identify, as accurately as possible, the feeling that is being communicated. To do this we must listen attentively and intently. We also observe body language and listen to tone of voice. (At this point, you may want to give a few example statements and ask participants to identify the feelings.)

– *The second step* is to accept the feeling that has been identified. There is a tendency, if we identify an unpleasant feeling, to try to find a solution to change the feeling. Remind participants that responsibility for finding solutions is the transmitter's and not theirs. Acceptance means to accept the reality of that feeling, that the feeling is real for the transmitter. Acceptance does not imply that the feeling is good or bad, right or wrong, logical or illogical; just that it exists and needs to be dealt with.

– *The third step* is to verbalize the feeling; to make a feedback statement to the transmitter in response to his statement. (Refer to the last diagram in the decoding process. You may want to add a few examples.)

4. **Feeling Word List**

   (The purpose of this is to make participants aware of and expand their feeling vocabulary.)

   Ask the group to brainstorm a list of feeling words. As they suggest feeling words, record them on the chalkboard or on newsprint. Point out that often we are not accustomed to using feeling words, and we are unaware of the many feeling words we know and the subtle shades of meaning they convey. When you decide to end the list, it may be interesting to compare the number of down feelings to the number of up feelings. (Usually people can think of more down feelings.) You may want to hand out the two Emotional Vocabulary sheets (Positive Feelings and Negative Feelings) included at the end of this section.

5. **Listening for Feeling Worksheet**

   Handout the worksheet and go through the exercises. Participants will complete their worksheets privately, then share their responses with the group. <u>Be sure to conclude the activity by reading or role-playing the examples of using Listening for Feeling with Slump Intervention activities.</u> Participants are learning to use the skill initially by practicing responses to simple, single statements. <u>But, the way we want them to use the skill is as a Slump Intervention technique.</u>

Roadblocks

ROADBLOCKS TO COMMUNICATION

(THIS SECTION ALSO KNOWN AS "TWELVE WAYS TO REALLY SCREW UP ANY RAPPORT YOU MIGHT HAVE DEVELOPED WITH YOUR SALESPEOPLE WHEN YOU ARE TRYING TO GET THEM TO "DO THEIR JOB.")

Suppose your salesperson is having a difficult time meeting higher sales quota. Somehow he lets the salesmanager know about this problem and that it is really bothering him. Here are some typical responses from the salesmanager that closes all avenues of communication:

1. **Ordering or commanding** – example – "Stop complaining and get your work done."
2. **Warning or threatening** – example – "You better shape up if you want to keep your job."
3. **Moralizing, preaching, giving "shoulds" and "oughts"** – example – "You know it's your job to sell the product." "You should leave your personal problems at home where they belong"
4. **Advising or offering solutions** – example – "The thing for you to do is to start working earlier." "Then you'll have more time for selling."
5. **Teaching, lecturing, giving logical arguments** – example – "Let's look at the facts." "You only have 15 more days to make your quota."

The above examples offer solutions to the salesperson. The next three examples communicate judgment, evaluation or put-downs.

6. **Judging, criticizing, disagreeing, blaming** – example – "You're either a complete goof-off or an accomplished procrastinator."
7. **Name-calling, stereotyping, labeling** – example – "You're acting like an adolescent, not like a pro representing this company."
8. **Interpreting, analyzing, diagnosing** – example – "What do you mean they won't give you appointments?" "You must be paranoid."

THE SALES SLUMP DOCTOR IS IN!

The next two messages are attempts by the salesmanager to make the salesperson feel better – to make the problem go away – or to deny that a problem exists.

9. **Praising, agreeing, giving positive evaluations** – example – "You're one heck of a salesperson." "I'm sure you'll figure out how to meet your quota."
10. **Reassuring, sympathizing, consoling, supporting** – example –"You're not alone when it comes to having a bad month." "I've experienced tough months, too." "Besides, when you start making sales again you'll roll right past your quota."

The next one is the most frequently used roadblock even though salesmanagers realize that questions often produce defensiveness. Also, questions are most often used when the salesmanager feels he needs more facts because he plans to solve the salesperson's problem by presenting the best of all possible solutions, rather than help the salesperson solve their own problem. (Give a person a fish and you feed him for a day. Teach a person to fish and you feed him for life.)

11. **Questioning, probing, interrogating, cross-examining** – example – "Do you think your quota is too high?" "How much time have you spent on it?" "Why did you wait so long to come to me?"

This last category consists of methods that salesmanagers use to change the subject, divert the salesperson, or avoid having to deal with the salesperson at all.

12. **Withdrawing, distracting, being sarcastic, humoring, diverting** – example – "Ah come on, can't we talk about something more pleasant?" "This is a bad time?" "Let's get back to making calls." "Seems like someone has a burr under their saddle today."

All of the dirty dozen tell the salesperson that you are non-accepting of their problem. This will stop any dialog in its tracks. Remember, the name of this article is *How do you get them to talk? You listen, listen listen!* But you also have to know how to listen. If you don't know what this means, go directly back to the beginning and re-read!

EMOTIONAL VOCABULARY

POSITIVE FEELINGS

MILD	MODERATE		STRONG	
merry	glad	jolly	thrilled	elated
good	cheerful	happy	joyful	
pleased	amused	delighted	successful	proud
interested	aroused	stimulated	enthusiastic	loved
			excited	
infatuated	warm	affectionate	idolized	loved
friendly	cared-for	liked	adored	
		popular		
alert	intense	vibrant	zestful	jubilant
				alive
				free
relaxed	complacent	calm	peaceful	tranquil
		contented		
		comfortable		
adventurous		daring	brave	courageous
	radiant		rapturous	
o.k.	confident	capable	determined	forceful
			positive	dedicated
safe		protected		secure
interested	attentive		involved	fascinated
attractive	coy	interesting	seductive	sexy
appealing		pretty		
active	energetic	enlivened	invigorated	
	perceptive		understanding	

THE SALES SLUMP DOCTOR IS IN!

EMOTIONAL VOCABULARY

NEGATIVE FEELINGS

MILD	MODERATE		INTENSE	
upset	fed up	mad	infuriated furious angry	irate, enraged, hostile, hateful
blue, down blah, sad, low	downcast sorrowful	forlorn dismayed	woeful gloomy despondent	dejected depressed
bashful	shy sensitive	embarrassed timid	hurt	humiliated rejected
concerned uncomfortable	scared uneasy	afraid frightened	horrified	terrified
on edge	troubled	worried	apprehensive	anxious
unimportant		inadequate	ineffectual	useless
puzzled	baffled mixed-up	unsure confused	bewildered	disoriented
	perplexed			overwhelmed panicky
edgy fidgety	jittered tense keyed-up	nervous shaky	uptight	out of control
impatient		frustrated		disgusted
	let-down	disappointed		
	distrustful		suspicious	
			helpless	desperate futile
		discouraged	dismayed	hopeless
tired	weary worn-out	listless	fatigued lethargic	exhausted
sorry		regretful	ashamed	guilty
hesitant	reluctant	skeptical	turned-off	
	competitive	envious	jealous	
	surprised	startled	shocked	astounded
unconcerned	disinterested	indifferent	ambivalent	apathetic
		bitter	resentful	revengeful
dislike		loathe	detest abhor	hate despise

Activities

LISTENING FOR FEELING: A GROUP DISCUSSION SKILL

"Listening for Feeling" is an effective group discussion skill to use while conducting training activities for Slump Intervention. The activities themselves are intended to stimulate participants to discuss and think about themselves and their own feelings and values in relation to a number of specific areas. "Listening for Feeling," because it is non-judgmental, encourages participants to speak freely and openly, without fear of criticism or rejection.

PURPOSE OF LISTENING FOR FEELING

1. It helps participants become aware of, identify, and accept their own feelings – The first step in learning to deal with feelings.
2. It encourages participants to express, reflect on, and clarify their own values.
3. It gives participants the opportunity to "air" their feelings and get them off their chest.
4. It boost participants' self-concept by making them feel important. (Using the skill requires the instructor to listen carefully to participants and to demonstrate verbally this careful listening. It makes anyone feel important to know his words are listened to carefully.)
5. It shows participants that they have the freedom to have and express their own feelings and values.

ACTIVITY 1 – IDENTIFYING FEELINGS

Directions: 1. Read each statement as though someone said it to you.
2. Identify and accept the feeling you hear.
3. Write the feeling in the space provided.

Practice Statements:

1. "I put together this presentation without any help."
   Identify feeling _____
2. "I wonder what this seminar will be like? I hope I do good."
   Identify feeling _____
3. "I can't wait until I can take my family on vacation!"
   Identify feeling _____
4. "Everyone in this group laughs at me when I ask questions."
   Identify feeling _____

THE SALES SLUMP DOCTOR IS IN!

5. "My paper work is so backed up that I don't believe I'll ever get it done."
   Identify feeling _____

ACTIVITY 2 – PRACTICING "LISTENING FOR FEELING" STATEMENTS

Now that you have learned to recognize feelings, the next step is to respond to the statements. Under each feeling you have identified in the previous 5 statements, write a complete "Listening for Feeling" sentence that you might use to respond to the speaker in a real situation. The incomplete sentences below may help you get started. Just add the feelings you have identified to the incomplete sentences. These are only suggestions and examples. Use you own style and expressions.

You feel _____
Sounds like *you* feel _____
You sound _____
You'd rather _____
It's important to *you* that _____
You like/don't like _____
You are _____

USING "LISTENING FOR FEELING" WHEN YOU ARE ACTUALLY DOING THE TRAINING

When doing training, "Listening for Feeling" is especially useful because it:
1. helps the instructor keep the discussion focused, thus preventing "bull sessions" and drifting off the subject.
2. tends to keep discussion on a personal level, with the result that participants take the discussions more seriously and maintain interest.
3. fosters participation among those participants who might normally have very little to say.

When participants express themselves, the instructor responds with a "Listening for Feeling" statement. This often results in the participant expressing himself further or clarifying his original statement. The instructor may then make another "Listening for Feeling" statement. The participant responds again. After a short series of these exchanges, the instructor moves on to another participant.

Practice this with your peers. Doing this will give you ideas to use when you are doing training and want to model this skill to the group.

APPENDIX

Energizers

USING ENERGIZERS

These simple and enjoyable games can serve a variety of purposes. The most obvious is that if used first thing in the morning, immediately after lunch, or even after a rather lengthy discussion, they help the group to "wake up" and become energized for the work to follow. They also provide an opportunity for the group to function together in a light activity that is generally non-threatening. In addition, the activity itself can be processed after it has been completed, providing another opportunity for the group, or the individuals, to become aware of the feelings and behaviors of others. And lastly, the importance of simply having fun is sometimes forgotten in a task-oriented group, and these activities provide the kind of break that all of us need. Let's jump right in and explore some exercises.

Back-to-Back

This is an energetic, fast paced exercise. Clear a space for the participants to move around in. Ask everyone to pick a partner and stand back-to-back with arms linked together. Everyone who wants to participate should be paired, except you, the "caller." Tell participants that you will call different positions, such as "knee-to-knee," "shoulder-to-shoulder," toe-to-toe," etc., and that they should move quickly to the position as you call it. When you call "back-to-back," they must find a new partner and stand back-to-back with elbows linked. The caller must also find a partner, and the person left without a partner becomes the new caller. Be sure to call the positions quickly, so the participants are moving more than they are standing still. Continue for about 5 minutes.

Knot

Ask the participants to get into a huddle. Ask each person to reach out and with each hand take someone else's hand. They should not take the hands of someone who is right next to them, and they should be holding hands with two different people, rather than taking both hands of one person. Once everyone is holding hands, the group must work together to unravel into one big circle without letting go of hands. Sometimes the group unravels into two circles.

Forced Choice

Indicate an imaginary line down the center of the room. As you ask each "either/or" question, point to the side of the line where participants who make that choice should stand. For example, "Are you a kite (point to one side of the line) or a clothes line (point to the other side of the line)?" After each question ask for one or two volunteers from each side to share their reasons for their choices. Move quickly through the list.

Are you . . .
- A kite or a clothesline
- The country or the city
- The mountains or the beach
- A jeep or a Cadillac
- A ski lift cable or a telephone line
- A quill pen or a type writer
- A spender or a saver
- Summer or winter
- Yes or no
- A tortoise or a hare
- Patent leather or suede.

Double Circle Exercise

(Purpose: to help participants become acquainted; to share feelings about the program, workshop, training session, etc., to get participants moving and involved.)

1. Ask participants to number off – 1, 2, 1, 2, etc. All 1's form a circle facing out. All 2's form a circle around 1's so that each 2 is facing a 1. Ask the following questions, allow a few minutes for each person in the "pairs" to answer. Then blow a whistle and outside persons (the 2's) take one step to the right. Ask a new question.

   Suggested Questions:
   - How did you hear about this workshop?
   - How would you spend $100,000 (tax free)?
   - How do you feel about using the slump intervention techniques?
   - If you could pick a new first name, what would it be?
   - How do you feel about being at this workshop?
   - What is one thing you would like to change about yourself?
   - What is something you like about yourself?

2. Process the circle exercise for participants as "trainers." Go over the purpose of the exercise. Ask how they would use this exercise in

THE SALES SLUMP DOCTOR IS IN!

their sales organization. How would they modify the questions for their salespeople? Point out that it is a good idea to mix sales related (or task related) questions with personal questions.

3. This is the time to distribute handouts you will be using early in the workshop, if any, and explaining their uses to the group. At this point they can ask questions about the handouts and make their own notes relating to the handouts.

Name Tag Exercise

(Purpose: to help participants get acquainted, to raise questions relevant to being a salesperson, to illustrate an activity from the program guide, if one is used.)

1. Pass out 5" x 8" blank cards or half sheets of colored construction paper, straight pins, and felt tip pens or crayons. Ask participants to write the name they want to be called during the workshop in the center of the card and embellish it as they wish. They should leave room to put other information about themselves on the card.

2. Give the following instructions (or make up your own items), leaving time after each instruction for participants to complete:

    - List five qualities of a good salesperson or salesmanager around your name.
    - In top right corner, put name of a person who has had an impact on you.
    - In top left corner, put a skill (personal or professional) you would like to have or to improve.
    - Across bottom, complete the sentence: "The most important thing I can do as a salesperson or salesmanager is _____."

3. Ask participants to mill around for a few minutes and to silently read each other's nametags.

4. Ask participants to form triads and share nametags (about 5 minutes). Discussion could be based on clarifying questions such as: "Who is the person who influenced your life and how are you different because of this person? How could you get or improve the skill you listed? Why are your five qualities of a good salesperson or

salesmanager important to you — how did you come to choose these qualities? What were the reasons for your answer to 'the most important thing I can do as a salesperson or salesmanager?'" (You may want to post these questions on a flip chart or chalkboard.)

5. At the end of the discussion, ask each person to write on the back of his/her nametag: "One thing I learned about myself is _____ " or "One thing I relearned about myself is _____." Ask volunteers to share "I learned" statements.

6. Process exercise. Go over purpose. Ask participants how they could use this activity in their sales organizations — what purpose could it serve? Brainstorm other items that could be included on the nametag.

Selected Start-Ups and Introduction Activities

The activities suggested below are generally helpful in at least three ways:
1. As ice breakers;
2. To help participants get to know who something about each other;
3. To help identify group members as possible future resources.

And besides, these activities are fun. This list is just a beginning, and the length of your own list will grow with your experiences.

1. **Paired Introductions**
   Each person meets and gets to know one other person and in turn introduces his partner to the entire group.

2. **Dyad (Pair) and Quartet**
   Same as above, but instead of introducing his partner to the entire group, he introduces him to another dyad.

3. **One-Minute Autobiography**
   Break into groups of a dozen or so. Each person is given one minute to tell about himself. Use a timekeeper, and don't let anyone go over one minute. Restrictions can be set as to what can be talked about (e.g., nothing about job, family, home town, hobbies). These restric- tions enable the participants to get right to attitudes and values.

4. **Depth Unfolding Process**
   a. Use in small groups, because it takes five minutes per person.

THE SALES SLUMP DOCTOR IS IN!

    b. Leader discloses first to aid in trainee comfort.
    c. In the first three minutes, tell what has brought you to this point in your life. One minute is used to describe your happiest moment. The last minute is used to answer questions from others.

5. **Structured Introductions**

    In dyads, small groups, or in the large group, participants can talk about their happiest moment, write their own epitaphs, write a press release about themselves, etc.

6. **Life Map**

    Each person draws, on newsprint with crayons or magic markers, a picture of his life using stick figures and symbols.

7. **Name Circle**

    Participants sit in a large circle. The leader begins by stating the name of the person seated to his right, followed by his own name. The person to his right repeats the leader's name, his own name, and then adds the name of the person seated to his right. This process is repeated around the entire circle.

8. **Sandwich Boards**

    Each person writes on a sheet of newsprint "Things I Know" (about the content and purpose of the workshop, areas of personal expertise, etc.). On a second sheet of newsprint, he writes "Things I Want to Know." The sheets are joined with tape sandwich board style, and the participants mill around, non-verbally, identifying resources and getting to know one another.

9. **Consensus Based Group Objectives**

    Each person privately lists five (the number is optional) personal objectives for the workshop. He shares them with a partner, and they arrive at five. The dyads go to quartets and then to octets. The octets report out their objectives (reached by consensus) and a total group set of objectives is formulated. This activity can aid in checking the contract and also help obviate the problem of hidden agendas.

10. **Sentence Completions**

    A prepared list of sentences (Anyone who smokes in front of his children . . .) is spun around the group or used in small groups.

TIPS FOR TRAINERS

The following is a collection of ideas, suggestion and concerns, which may help the trainer in conducting workshops and provide helpful follow-up consultation. The list was drawn from many sources and certainly not exhaustive. The items included here have to do with trainer style, attitudes and answers to frequently asked questions.

1. The need for careful attention to detail when planning the workshop cannot be over emphasized. Have materials and equipment in place in advance. Decide how subgroups will be formed, when to give instructions, when to distribute handouts. Plan the responsibilities of each trainer (if more than one trainer is used), and know when each takes over or intervenes in an activity.

2. Timing is of the essence. Plan a schedule, which is realistic, and plan to stick to it. If the group's needs dictate a change, know ahead of time where you can add or subtract time from planned activities, and still meet your objectives. Start on time; trainers model promptness!

3. The best workshop results occur when trainers work together as a team, as opposed to each trainer showing up for his particular session and then leaving. The team relationship, and each trainer staying involved throughout the workshop, helps to build rapport between the trainers and the participants. Also, with all trainers present, those who are no on their feet can give back up to the person who is, and help him keep track of the time.

4. If you have a choice, here are some pros and cons on different scheduling formats. A two-day workshop is a more intense training session. Group rapport and comfort level build to higher points. On the other hand, participants are usually exhausted and saturated at the end of the second day. Breaking the workshop into 3 to 4 hour sessions spread over several days does not exhaust participants and gives them the opportunity to test activities in their offices between sessions. At the beginning of each session, it does take a little time to build back to the point where you left at the last session. This may not be a critical factor, however, when you are working only with

THE SALES SLUMP DOCTOR IS IN!

participants from the same office or company in the workshop.

5. Remember that this training is primarily experiential. Keep lectures to a minimum. (Many things we may want to tell participants they can learn more effectively for themselves.) Avoid lengthy discussions about small details. Encourage these participants to see you during breaks, after the workshop, etc.

6. At times you may encounter one or two participants in a workshop who want to continue to discuss an issue long after it has been resolved and holds no interest for the other workshop participants. It is important that they not be allowed to monopolize the workshop. Respond to their concerns, and explain that because of the tight schedule, it would be better to continue the discussion during break, after the workshop, etc.

7. Participants may sometimes resist new ideas or skills based on unsuccessful experiences in the field, lack of support from upper management, lack of confidence in their own ability, etc. A successful trainer and consultant must accept these feelings of negativism, doubt, resistance, lack of support, etc., before he can successfully build self-confidence and encourage the innate creativity in participants. This is a good time to model active listening skills!

8. Some participants will resist the concept of using Slump Intervention techniques and your suggestions despite your earnest efforts. Concentrate on helping those participants who have a desire to try Slump Intervention techniques. The others will eliminate themselves through self-selection; that is, they won't use the material; therefore, they won't stay with the program if it doesn't work for them.

9. Be very supportive of any small steps in learning and motivation. Some participants will be slow to grasp the philosophy and concepts of Slump Intervention, but will give it a try and stick with it with your encouragement and support.

10. Always be alert to both verbal and non-verbal cues from the participants as to their understanding and acceptance of the program. When appropriate, respond to these in the workshop. When unsure of their needs, or when their cues suggest a problem of an individual nature, pursue these during breaks or soon after the workshop.

11. Avoid moralizing or defending. There are many ways to teach Slump Intervention techniques, and what is offered in the workshop is not the only way. Be willing to accept other views and values, but don't feel obligated to defend the ones you have chosen to be effective for you.

12. Be realistic in helping the participants move from the workshop experience back to the business world. The real world will not be as accepting and problem-free as is the workshop environment. They must recognize this and not expect instant success.

13. Participants are not asked to be therapists, but, with your help, they can learn to identify the salesperson or salesmanager with special needs and refer his for special help. Remember, the large majority of the salespeople or salesmanagers don't need therapy, just a little assistance in growing beyond their learned limitation.

14. Keep a mailing list of participants. Keep them informed of similar workshops that are being offered, through local organizations, if any.

15. A special note to team coordinators: Keep at least one other team member as aware as you are of any plans you have negotiated to implement the Slump Intervention Program in your area. If, for any reason, you should leave the team, they will have a good handle on the program and can carry on.

About the Author

"Sparklers, 5¢ a box and six for a quarter!" And with that singsong lilt, the Sales Slump Doctor launched his selling career at age 5. He sold sparklers, cap guns, and caps from a pasteboard box on Broughton Street in Johnny Mercer's Savannah, Georgia, during the Christmas holidays from school. When it wasn't sparkler season, he was collecting pasteboard boxes in the alley behind retail stores and selling them to Nugent's Bakery, or collecting coat hangers and selling them to Gay's Dry Cleaners. Pennies were hard to come by in those days — but they went real far! But let's get back to the start of this story. (NOTE: I will leave the third person description and go to first person.)

To begin, I was born the fourth of five on February 20, 1932. Julie was the oldest. Then there was Leonard, Gerald. Stanley came 7 years later. When I consider that 1932 was in the midst of the Great Depression, it makes me wonder if I was planned. Oh well, accidents cause people. I do remember once asking my father if he had ever been slipped a Mickey and he said, "Yes, when you were born."

Julie was born with part of her brain extruding just above the nose and between the eyes. The doctor operated and she lived (a miracle for 1921), but she was paralyzed and retarded. Her mental capacity was less than that of a two year old. This put quite a strain on the family, and I guess you might say we were dysfunctional. We did not know it, but we were quite ahead of our times. Dysfunctional families didn't become fashionable until much, much later.

We grew up poor, and we knew it. Most of the money my dad earned as assistant manager of Sears and Roebuck went to feed this hungry crew, and anything that was left was used for Julie. She was also epileptic and had frequent grand mat seizures.

I remember one day when I was eight being alone in the house with Julie when she had a seizure. She sat in a cane rocking chair, and when the seizure began you had just a few seconds to get to her and place your leg between hers so that when she stiffened she would remain over the chair and not fall onto the floor. Then when she relaxed she would collapse back into the chair and would eventually recover.

As I said, I was only eight years old and still quite light in the butt. The seizure began and I rushed to the rescue. I placed my right leg between her stiffening legs and before I knew it we were both on the floor. I lay there with her until the seizure passed feeling like a helpless failure.

Kindergarten was fun, and I could not wait to go to school. Miss Reddy was my first grade teacher and she was ancient — or so I thought. However, she did teach until I was about to graduate from high school. Guess she wasn't as old as she appeared to this six year old.

I did well in grammar school and began to wane in junior high. The teachers thought my interests went in other directions and blamed that for my poor grades. High school was a disaster. I was socially promoted and graduated one semester later than scheduled. I did extremely well in biology lab, math, and other non-reading courses, but utterly failed all reading courses. I developed an almost photographic auditory recall, and that allowed me to graduate just one semester late. It wasn't until later that I discovered I had a learning disability, and I will cover this in due course.

Throughout high school I boxed at the Union Bag Athletic Association. I wasn't great, but I was pretty good. When you grow up with two older brothers you have to be good to survive. Remember, all this was before television, and beating up little brother was great amusement.

Early on I was interested in working. Aside from selling sparkiers, pasteboard boxes, and coat hangers, when I was seven or younger, I remember going to my grandfather's little grocery store in Yamacraw every Sunday morning to work. I waited on the children who were sent to shop for their parents. Naturally, I was assigned menial tasks, but I really wanted to chop neck bones like Uncle Harry. He was my hero behind the meat counter, but every time I tried to imitate him they would all hurry over to take the meat cleaver from me. How was I to learn if they wouldn't let me try? Today, I understand their fears, but then it was a real puzzle.

In December of 1945 I went to work for the Christmas Season at S and G Men's Shop. It was a very fashionable men's clothing store in a predominately Afro-American area of town. I fell madly in love with the business and my dream for the future was to own such a store. Getting this job was no small task. Bobby Gordon, the son of the owner, had just returned from the war where he was a bombardier in the European Theater of Operation, and he was the one I had to convince to hire me. He asked me to stand behind the counter and then told me to come back next year. I did not understand this. Here I was ready to work and they didn't want me. What kind of world was this anyway?

During the pursuing week I saw Bobby at the gym and he told me he couldn't hire me because no one could see me behind the counter. I told him

I would come out from behind the counter to wait on customers, and he told me to come to work next Saturday. I did and remained there until I graduated from high school. They were wonderful people and taught me a lot about business.

When I graduated from high school in 1950 I decided it was time to get into the big times. Time to move to Broughton Street where all the leading stores operated. I went to work for B. K., the owner of a very upscale men's clothing store. He was a tough taskmaster and for that I am grateful. If he had been the slightest bit nice I would never have gone to school. I credit him for sending me (and probably many others) to college in order to escape the likes of him.

This job was short lived. The Navy Reserves thought my presence was needed during the Korean Conflict and I was called to active duty. It was during this period while stationed at Bethesda Naval Hospital that I learned that I could not read. I was in the Mellon Art Gallery with Roselyn C., a Corp Wave, and asked her a question. She looked at me and said, "Mickey, you can't read, can you?" It took me by surprise, but I answered honestly and told her that I didn't think so. To this day I do not know what she did, but in a few weeks I was able to read a book and remember what I read. The name of the book was Once Around the Park by Michael Shannon. It was the very first book I read from cover to cover and I was 20 years old.

I was released form active duty in December of 1953 with an insatiable thirst for knowledge. I entered Armstrong Junior College and was lucky enough to be exposed to Orson Beecher, Hinkle Murphy and Joseph Killorin. These were three great philosophers who used the Socratic method of teaching. We didn't study dates in history, we studied the great minds of that period. The same was true for English Literature. It was a great educational experience for someone just learning to read and who was thirsting for knowledge.

In my junior year I went to the University of Georgia and became a philosophy major. I was on the G. I. Bill and had to comply with what the V. A. ordered. They wanted me to take the law school entrance exam, but I told them I wanted to teach philosophy. They said they knew that but that they needed to show that they were working with me. I took the exam and after several weeks the Dean of the Law School asked me to come see him. He told me he would exempt my senior year of undergraduate work if I would enter Law School in September. For a kid who was socially promoted in high school I was indeed flattered and went to Law School.

The G. I. Bill was not enough to live on and my family did not have the means to supplement this income so I chose to work. The first year in Law School I worked at Watson's Drug Store where I sold everything from sodas to sanitary napkins. Towards the end of that year I got a better job working for G. Fain Slaughter at the Athens Credit Bureau. He was quite a gentleman and helped me immensely. Law School was from 8:00 a.m. to 12:50 p.m. on Mondays through Fridays, and the job at the Credit Bureau was from 1:00 p.m. until 5:00 p.m. The following year I began also managing the Pig Restaurant from 5:30 p.m. to midnight. I could study when things slowed down around 9:00 p.m. until closing time.

I began dating Sonia Robbins during my first year in Law School. She was a sophomore in the School of Education also at the University of Georgia. We dated just about every night for a full nine months and never kissed. We were great friends. Every one else knew we were in love except us. Then one day it hit us and I fled the scene. It scared me to death. I did come back just before the summer vacation and we decided that if our relationship survived the summer we would probably get married. We did just that on July 7, 1957. Last July 7 we celebrated our 43rd anniversary with our three daughters, their husbands, and our 5 grand children.

I loved the study of law and graduated in June of 1958. I soon joined a firm of general practioners as a law clerk, but could not stand what I was doing. I always thought we represented the wrong party. I was doing things to people and not for people and that was not my style.

When we graduated, Sonia from the School of Education and me from Law School, Sonia was six months pregnant. Sharon was born on September 10, 1958, and I was in Atlanta taking the Bar Exam. I left before it was over to come home to my first-ever baby and determined to get back to Atlanta in February to re-take the exam. Before February came Sonia was again pregnant and beginning to miscarry which took place during her sixth month. All this was very traumatic on our young family and I wasn't making any money. I needed a job.

The General Agent for Pilot Life frequently gave me a ride home after work. One day he noticed my depressed demeanor and asked what was wrong. I told him, and he suggested we meet for breakfast the next day. We did and in short order I became an agent for Pilot Life at the starting draw of $300 per month plus a percentage of my earnings in excess of the draw. I always earned more than the draw, but still could only get a percentage of the excess. The rest was held for when I went off the draw. Meanwhile, Sonia and I were expecting again. I asked the General Agent if I could get a few hundred dollars of my draw to buy some baby furniture for the new baby who was expected in November of 1960. He assured me that I would get the money and I went in debt for the things we needed for the baby. Just before the baby arrived the General Agent told me the company would not release the money. I was irate to say the least!

THE SALES SLUMP DOCTOR IS IN!

Coincidental to these events, Harold T. Dillon, General Agent for the National Life of Vermont, contacted me and wanted me to fly to Atlanta to speak with him. I informed him that my wife was expecting any day and that I was not going to be in Atlanta again when my child was born. He agreed and flew into Savannah to see me. Meanwhile Lori was born and when Harold arrived the first thing he asked was, "Has the baby been born?" When I told him she was born yesterday he insisted that I stop by the florist shop and he sent Sonia a bouquet of orchids. Boy, I was impressed.

We went to his hotel room and met for several hours. He then said, "I want you," to which I responded, "We haven't spoken of money yet." He said, "You don't understand, I said I want you and money is secondary." I then explained my predicament and instead of a few hundred he sent me a few thousand. His theory was that if he wanted you to be a big league salesperson he had to treat you like a big league salesperson.

I remember not making the MDRT in 1961, my first year with the Dillon-Griffin Agency, and I vowed that would never happen again — It didn't. I learned a great deal about business insurance and began specializing in selling to closely held corporations. They were usually family-owned and there were many tax benefits when using the company to purchase the insurance. It wasn't long before my premium production ranged from $150,000 to $250,000 per year.

After Harold retired in 1964 things began to change and I decided that at my premium income level I could afford to become a personal producing general agent. Wow! My personal income really jumped. I continued doing this until 1975.

Meanwhile, my drinking, which began when I was a very young teenager, began to be a problem. It seemed that everything would get in the way of my drinking which continued to escalate. At this point I was beginning to drink daily and blacked out often. Sonia thought this was due to being unhappy in the insurance business and suggested going back to school to study psychology. I went back to school and the drinking continued. Soon cocaine was added and I was really off to the races.

During 1981 and 1982 I taught Sales and Psychology at South College of Savannah. I loved it but it interfered with my psychotherapy practice so I quit.

I completed my masters level course work and was accepted into a doctoral program. That is where I did my research on the slump intervention. Prior to this I did have the opportunity to treat several insurance agents who were suffering from sales slumps. This was going good, but I needed the time to work and study and drink.

In 1983 Bayard Publishers in Stamford, Conn. heard about my work asked me to write a book on my theory of using crisis intervention techniques to treat the sales slump. I never took it seriously, and besides, it got in the way of my drinking.

I completed my doctoral program in January of 1984, and had a somewhat active practice of psychotherapy. In 1986 I went into treatment for my alcohol and drug addiction problems and then returned to my general practice. I continued to do this until 1987, when I decided to specialize in the treatment of chemical dependency. I founded the Greenfield Center in Savannah, Georgia, moved it to Jacksonville, Florida, a year and a half later, and am still running the program.

About three years ago I was cleaning out some old files, and came across my dissertation. I read it after not even thinking about it for many years and discovered that it was good! I wrote a few articles that were published in Financial Services Advisor, which led to becoming an Editor-at-Large on this magazine. With encouragement from Fred Kissling and others at Lexington House, these articles and my dissertation became this book.

THE SALES SLUMP DOCTOR IS IN!

Notes

THE SALES SLUMP DOCTOR IS IN!

Notes

THE SALES SLUMP DOCTOR IS IN!

Notes

Notes

First Check Your Local Bookstore For This Important New Title.

This Book Profiles the Greatest Best-Selling Motivators of All Time!

Jack Canfield, Co-Author of
The #1 *New York Times* Best-Seller
Chicken Soup for the Soul
Wrote Three Chapters In
Forrest Wallace Cato's
What It Takes To Make You Great!
This is the only book in which
America's Three <u>Best-Selling</u> Motivators for Sales & Success
Offer You Timeless Success Secrets!

What It Takes To Make You Great!

The syndicated column **Best-in-Books** reported, "This work is certain to be an international self-help and personal development best-seller!"

Norman Vincent Peale	W. Clement Stone	Robert H. Schuller
Positive Thinking	*Positive Mental Attitude*	*Possibility Thinking*

Contains an Introduction by Rev. Dr. John Clements
The Best-Selling Inspirational Writer in Great Britain

Brian Tracy on America's Three Great Motivators:

"Norman Vincent Peale ranks among the most inspirational speakers of all time. His books and messages are timeless motivators for everyone!"

"W. Clement Stone motivated and inspired an entire generation of salespeople and entrepreneurs to great success!"

"Robert H. Schuller is the master of possibility thinking, a wonderful storyteller, and a great messenger of success!"

Oral Roberts on America's Three Great Motivators:

"Norman Vincent Peale, to me, was the right kind of salesman! His enthusiasm for life and positive spirit toward me almost swept me off my feet!"

"W. Clement Stone I know very well, having been in his home, his office, speaking to his sales staff, and having him speak at Oral Roberts University where he motivated our students and faculty! I value this salesman above all others!"

"Robert H. Schuller has the gift of inspiring millions world wide, spiritually and literally. He has touched my life. He can touch your life!"

Art Linkletter on America's Three Great Motivators:

"Norman Vincent Peale touched my life like no other, with a spirit and a light that will never fade. I think of him in times of trouble!"

"W. Clement Stone inspired me to never give up! He told me 'Decide what you want out of life and never give up until you have achieved it!'"

"Robert H. Schuller is an inspiration. He is the rightful inheritor of the Peale role in the gospel of positive thinking."

$22.95

Contributors to
What It Takes To Make You Great!
Include:
- Steve Allen
- Mary Kay Ash
- Jack Canfield
- Deepak Chopra
- Rev. Dr. John Clements
- Robert Dames
- Wayne W. Dyer
- Sidney A. Friedman
- Roy M. Henry
- Lou Holtz
- Tom Hopkins
- Edmund C. Hughes
- Barry Kaye
- Fred R. Kissling, Jr.
- Jack La Lanne
- Art Linkletter
- Anthony Robbins
- T.R. Shantha, MD, PhD
- George F. Sterne
- Blair Singer
- David K. Straight
- Alvin Toffler
- Brian Tracy
- Denis E. Waitley
- The Ultimate Warrior
- Thomas R. Winter
- Zig Ziglar

and many more!

Lexington House
98 Dennis Drive
Lexington, KY 40503
1-800-356-5936
Fax 606-277-8059

Act Now! Order your copy using the Action Order Form at back of book.

Lexington House

First Check Your Local Book Retailer

No writer can touch your heart like the Rev. Dr. John Clements!

His major new book...

Make Your Walls Tumble

How To Change Your Impossible to Merely Difficult – Then Achieve Success!

...is sure to be a best-seller!

Rev. Dr. John Clements

Very many people – including some of world's most successful life-coaches and writers – are now describing the Reverend Dr. John Clements as "England's answer to the late Rev. Dr. Norman Vincent Peale" (inventor of the concept of positive thinking). Reverend Clements has been a success coach and mentor for (in his own words), "more years than I care to count," and, in *Make Your Walls Tumble,* he presents the reader with a whole *universe* of new possibilities for relationships, careers, and matters of the spirit – all underpinned by his own experience. "Fulfillment," says the good Doctor, "does not derive from *manipulating* but from *empowering;* success is not defined by *getting on* but by *getting honest;* contentment will be achieved not by a human *doing* but by a human *being.*"

The wellspring of inspiration for this book was the Reverend's home city of Norwich, England – a place with a history stretching back well before the Roman invasion of Britain. Many famous people have lived and left their mark around and within its ancient walls: Horatio Nelson, victor of Trafalgar; Nurse Edith Cavell, heroine of World War I; Elizabeth Fry, prison reformer; Lord Erpingham, the military leader who fired the first arrow at the Battle of Agincourt and subsequently gave his name to one of Norwich Cathedral's ancient gates...

...and many other characters you'll read about, and be inspired by, when you decide to *Make Your Walls Tumble.*

Naturally, the Reverend Doctor gets inspired to pen new reminiscences, stories, anecdotes and allegories every single time he walks though the historic streets of Norwich. And the book's structure reflects this, each chapter being prefaced by a one-page introduction inspired by an inhabitant or feature of the city, past or present. Indeed, it's no exaggeration to say that wisdom fairly gushes from every chapter.

"May God and Saint Monacella Be With You!" gives potted biographies of various historical characters, and analyses how their respective influences continue to ripple through space and time, still affecting the human race even centuries later.

"You Can Think Like a Fish!" whisks us back to the author's youth, when he never thought twice about taking risks; and the reader is asked: "If we now fail, is it because we've learned to be afraid? And if so, of what?"

"Your Easily-Bribed Gatekeepers!" compares the old walls of Norwich with the Great Wall of China, which ultimately proved useless for its defensive purpose – not because the invaders possessed massive engines of war, or even very tall ladders, but because the sentries at the gates were too human to resist...well, you can guess what!

Norwich is a city *steeped* in history. Its first Bishop, who began his ministry in 1096, would have been mightily impressed to read the sentiments in this volume. How do we know? Because the seventy-first Bishop has said *he's* mightily impressed! Part of his endorsement reads: "Norwich's churches sing their gospel praise through their very stones. But there are living stones as well...I thank God that he has raised up new witnesses like John Clements in this generation..."

Could there be a more persuasive acknowledgement of the Reverend Doctor's credentials?

Or a more heart-touching affirmation of his skill and power on the printed page?

Or a more powerful incentive to change your *impossible* to merely *difficult* – and then achieve success?

It's time to *Make Your Walls Tumble!*
Once you have read this book, you have the power...

Make Your Walls Tumble is published by:

Lexington House
98 Dennis Drive
Lexington, KY 40503
1-800-356-5936
Fax 606-277-8059

Use the Action Order Form at back of book to order your copy.